THE
INSIDER'S GUIDE
TO POLITICAL INTERNSHIPS

THE
INSIDER'S GUIDE
TO POLITICAL INTERNSHIPS

What to Do Once You're in the Door

EDITED BY

Grant Reeher and **Mack Mariani**

Westview
PRESS

A Member of the Perseus Books Group

Copyright © 2002 by Westview Press, A Member of the Perseus Books Group

Westview Press books are available at special discounts for bulk purchases in the United States by corporations, institutions, and other organizations. For more information, please contact the Special Markets Department at the Perseus Books Group, 11 Cambridge Center, Cambridge MA 02142, or call (617) 252-5298.

Published in 2002 in the United States of America by Westview Press, 5500 Central Avenue, Boulder, Colorado 80301-2877, and in the United Kingdom by Westview Press, 12 Hid's Copse Road, Cumnor Hill, Oxford OX2 9JJ

Find us on the World Wide Web at www.westviewpress.com

A Cataloging-in-Publication data record for this book is available from the Library of Congress.
ISBN 0-8133-4016-0
The paper used in this publication meets the requirements of the American National Standard for Permanence of Paper for Printed Library Materials Z39.48–1984.

10   9   8   7   6   5   4   3   2   1

To our future interns,
Jack and **Molly Mariani,**
and **Davis Reeher**

Contents

Boxes and Figures

Boxes

Figures

Acronyms

AA	administrative assistant
CBO	Congressional Budget Office
CEA	Council of Economic Advisors
CEQ	Council on Environmental Quality
CFR	*Code of Federal Regulations*
CIA	Central Intelligence Agency
CRS	Congressional Research Service
DEA	Drug Enforcement Administration
EEOB	Eisenhower Executive Office Building
EOP	Executive Office of the President
EPA	Environmental Protection Agency
FAIR	Federal Activities Inventory Reform (Act)
FAR	Federal Acquisition Regulations
FAR	Federal Aviation Regulations
FBI	Federal Bureau of Investigation
FDA	Food and Drug Administration
FDIC	Federal Deposit Insurance Corporation
FEMA	Federal Emergency Management Agency
FTR	Federal Travel Regulations
GAO	General Accounting Office
GPO	Government Printing Office
GSA	General Services Administration
LA	legislative assistant
LC	legislative correspondent
LD	legislative director

LIS	Legislative Information System
LOC	Library of Congress
NARA	National Archives and Records Administration
NASA	National Aeronautics and Space Administration
NSC	National Security Council
NSEE	National Society for Experiential Education
OA	Office of Administration
OMB	Office of Management and Budget
ONDCP	Office of National Drug Control Policy
OPM	Office of Personnel Management
OSTP	Office of Science and Technology Policy
OVP	Office of the Vice President
PAC	political action committee
USPS	U.S. Postal Service
VA	Veterans Affairs

Foreword

One of my favorite phrases I use to warn students when starting an internship is, "The world doesn't stop because an intern has come on board!" Starting an internship on an academic calendar schedule when an office is already busy with its own internal schedule can be like trying to get on a fast moving carousel without falling off. You think, "Will someone teach me what I need to know? Will I get feedback when I have questions? What if I do something wrong or embarrassing? What if I break the copy machine or accidentally hang up on a member of Congress? What if there are too many interns in the office, and I don't have enough to do? What if I am ignored or not given meaningful assignments?"

All legitimate concerns, but the secret to success for any internship is to consider the endeavor as a process that starts the moment you think about the idea of doing an internship. It means thinking about what you want to learn from an internship and preparing yourself for the relevant tasks.

Last summer I was asked by a reporter to estimate the number of interns in Washington, D.C. My answer was that it depends upon how you define the term. Does an intern have to be a student? Does an intern have to get academic credit? Does an intern have to be an unpaid volunteer? Does an intern have to work a certain number of hours?

The term *intern* has traditionally been used in the field of medical education, when a young medical student is given an apprenticeship at a hospital or other medical facility. Later, as the field of public administration matured, the use of the term intern was often utilized instead of the term apprentice to enhance the prestige of a person interested in learning about practical politics.

In 1970, Bernard Hennessey, one of the first political scientists to write about the theory of political internships, identified three critical elements in the definition of an internship: a real work situation, not a "simulation"; an opportunity to participate on the same basis as other workers; and an opportunity for systematic and continuous evaluation of the experience in order to develop some generalizations about politics. All three must be present in order for an experience to be considered a true internship. The concern to define an internship was partially in response to the growing unrest on college campuses and the demand by students to make the curriculum more relevant and practical, and by faculty concerns to distinguish an internship from a job.

During the 1970s, organizations such as the National Society for Experiential Education (NSEE) were formed to promote greater professionalism in the field among both faculty and practitioners to ensure a high quality experience. The annual meetings of NSEE bring together an increasing number of educators, site sponsors, and students who share information about innovative programs, approaches, and trends within the profession. It is not unusual to see elementary and high school teachers along with college professors, career center staff, and student affairs personnel discussing the issues and responsibilities of off-campus education.

In 1975 Bill and Sheila Burke of the University of Massachusetts at Amherst created what is now called The Washington Center for Internships and Academic Seminars, the first nonprofit organization solely dedicated to serving the higher education community by providing full service internship placement, academic programming, evaluation, and housing for college students. A pioneer in the use of the academic internship portfolio, The Washington Center requires full documentation of each intern's experience in order to recommend a passing grade to the intern's home institution.

In the mid to late 1990s, the American Political Science Association nurtured the development of an Organized Section of Experiential Education, composed of faculty who were interested in the education and training of students involved in various forms of participatory learning, such as internships, study abroad, service learning and simulations. The section has evolved into a significant group called the Organized Section on Undergraduate Education, chaired most recently by Dr. Reeher, one of the editors of this book. Through panel and paper presentations at academic meetings, the section has revealed a richness of approaches, expertise, and innovation that today serve as models of experiential education.

The internship of the 21st century is on a higher professional level because of a number of factors, not the least of which is the increasing number of former interns who now seek interns for their own organizations and provide for them a better experience than the "go-fer" days of their past when academic credit was not so easily awarded or expected. Since colleges have moved away from the idea of career "placement" (and the responsibility of finding jobs for its graduates) to providing career "development services," internships, cooperative education, and even service learning have taken on a higher degree of visibility and support on campus. Today many career development offices have a staff member dedicated to advising students on how to find and make the most of an internship. Part of the responsibility may be to help the student find a qualified professor to grant them credit for the internship. Clearly, the evolving institutional professionalism has meant that more students take internships more seriously, and thus need to be better prepared to be successful.

This fact brings me to why this book is so important in today's educational environment. The academic model seems to work best when there is a strong level of institutional support for an intern both on campus as well as in the city or town where the internship is located. Walking into an internship without being prepared, without having someplace to turn if things turn sour, or without having the proper mentoring can turn a big investment into a major loss of time, money, and educational opportunity.

Reeher and Mariani have assembled a series of essential chapters that help prepare interns for a variety of placements. In Part 1, both the editors and Cammarano emphasize the importance of making the most of the experience, by looking at it as a serious academic exercise that has implications for the study of political behavior. Using examples, they give advice about how to assess the various kinds of internships and how best to utilize them for educational value.

Political science classes that emphasize the practical side of politics will find the comparison of the various kinds of internships in Part 2 to be an interesting way to develop generalizations about various kinds of internships and about politics, from the national to the state and local levels. For probably the first time in print, serious attention is paid to internships in the Congressional district office, the executive branch, and nonprofit organizations. Being able to see beyond the internship to generalize about organizational structure and behavior, and the impact of the organization within the political system, helps to make the experience a more educational exercise.

Also, this section is ideal for a scope and methods of political science course that discusses careers for majors. Understanding the various kinds of positions, roles, and qualifications of various staff members can be useful not only for the pursuit of a particular career, but also for deciding where or with whom one wants to intern.

But choosing a quality internship and getting a quality experience are two different matters. How do you make yourself competitive? Being able to hit the ground running means at least being familiar with the work of an office and perhaps having skills other interns don't. Part 3 will give any political intern a good head start when it comes to referencing government documents and public policy sources. Keep this book in your top desk drawer so that when the research assignments are handed out, you'll know exactly where to turn for help.

Interns need good writing and communication skills to make themselves worthy of a quality internship, but the application of these skills in an actual political environment can throw a political science major off-balance. Unless you've taken courses in speech communications, public relations, and journalism, you'll need the instructions in Part 4 on how to write press releases, constituent letters, memoranda, and speeches. Then there are the constituent letters that many interns are first assigned to write to determine how savvy they are. When it comes to understanding public policy issues, being able to explain them in a few succinct paragraphs is a special talent. Try watching a congressional hearing on C-SPAN and then write a press release, a short staff memo or even a prepared statement by an imaginary congressman. It is not as easy as it sounds. You'll find that this section will help you pass your first test as an intern!

And finally, don't just take the authors' word for what it is like to be prepared for an internship. Read in Part 5 what former interns have to say and the advice they give. You'll see that it reinforces the advice throughout the book. What you'll find is that knowing what you want to do for an internship will help you to choose wisely because you'll recognize what you want to learn from your experience. Remember, you are looking for a balance between learning from and contributing to an office. Being prepared with a basic knowledge of who does what in an office, what you want to do in the office and how to do the kinds of things you are interested in will help you to go far.

In other words, an internship should not be a job. It should be a learning experience that helps you appreciate the value of your education and apply it to professional tasks and responsibilities. Being prepared to jump onto the carousel means you'll have the strength to hold on and to quickly get a feel for the pace and tempo of an organization. Preparation and insight will give you the balance you need to get your bearing and be a successful intern. Before you know it, you'll be supervising the other interns in the office!

Eugene J. Alpert, Ph. D.
Washington, D.C.
May 2002

Acknowledgments

This book would not exist without the work of the contributors, and so we thank them first. At all stages of the project, we benefited from the support, enthusiasm, and constructive criticism of many colleagues. Among those in particular are Gene Alpert, Ron Anderson, Pam Baker, Joe Cammarano, Paul Cole, Kathryn Doherty, Chris Downing, Rob Gavin, Jean Griffin, John Halldow, Glen Halva-Neubauer, William Hudson, Jill Leonhardt, The Honorable Susan Molinari, Andrew Moore, Dawn Nettnin, Kelli O'Connor, Eugene Patrone, The Honorable Tom Reynolds, Justin Roj, Kathryn Sowards, and Jeff Stonecash.

At Westview Press, we were fortunate to have the support, encouragement, and guidance of Steve Catalano, Holly Hodder, Trish Goodrich, Katharine Chandler, and Steven Baker. This book is better because of them. In preparing the manuscript, we were saved by Kelly Bogart's competence, efficiency, and good humor.

Finally, Reeher would like to thank Mariani for generating the original idea for the book, for asking him to join in the effort to produce it, and for the good collegiality and friendship along the way. Mariani would like to thank Reeher for saying yes, for his collegiality and friendship in return, and for keeping things on schedule. Both thank their families for everything else.

About the Editors
and Contributors

About the Editors

Grant Reeher is associate professor of political science and director of undergraduate studies at the Maxwell School of Citizenship and Public Affairs, Syracuse University. He is also senior research associate at the Maxwell School's Center for Policy Research. In addition, he is adjunct faculty in the Leadership for a Democratic Society program at the Federal Executive Institute, U.S. Office of Personnel Management. He chairs the American Political Science Association's Organized Section on Undergraduate Education and edits *The Political Science Educator.* His publications include *Narratives of Justice* (University of Michigan Press), *Education for Citizenship* (Rowman & Littlefield), and *Click on Democracy: The Internet's Power to Change Political Apathy into Civic Action* (Westview). His past employment includes a stint as staff member for U.S. Representative Norman D'Amours. He has supervised hundreds of interns over the years, both individually and through internship-based courses. He holds a Ph.D. in political science from Yale University.

Mack Mariani is director of special projects for the Monroe County (New York) Department of Communications and a Ph.D. candidate in political science at the Maxwell School of Citizenship and Public Affairs, Syracuse University. He is a former congressional aide to U.S. Representative Bill Paxon and a former legislative staff member for the Monroe County legislature. He began his legislative career as a congressional intern, first for U.S. Representative Jack Kemp and later for U.S. Representative Bill Paxon. He has served on the residence life staff of the Washington Center for Internships and Academic Seminars and has taught at Syracuse University, the State University of New York at Oswego, and Monroe Community College. His work has been published in *Legislative Studies Quarterly*, *Political Science Quarterly*, *Comparative State Politics*, and *Journal of Terrorism and Political Violence*. He is also coauthor of *Diverging Parties* (Westview).

About the Contributors

Eugene J. Alpert is senior vice president at The Washington Center for Internships and Academic Seminars, where he is in charge of academic affairs and student services. He is also president of the National Society for Experiential Education. He joined the Center in 1993, after teaching for many years at Texas Christian University. He received his Ph.D. from Michigan State University. He has served as an American Political Science Association Congressional Fellow, and has contributed articles to journals and books on legislative behavior.

Matthew Bennett is director of public affairs for Americans for Gun Safety (AGS), a nonprofit advocacy organization. Before coming to AGS, he served in the Clinton White House as deputy assistant to the president and deputy director of intergovernmental affairs. In that capacity, he was the president's principal liaison to the nation's governors, state legislators, state attorneys general, and other state elected officials. He previously served in the Office of the Vice President, where he was trip director and assistant counsel. As trip director he accompanied the vice president on all of his travels, both foreign and domestic, and helped during the trips to coordinate principal, staff, and press activity. He also participated in the planning of all public events involving the vice president. In addition, he provided legal counsel to the vice president and his staff on a range of issues. He supervised numerous interns in the White House.

Joseph Cammarano is assistant professor of political science at Providence College. He is also on the faculty of the Feinstein Institute for

Public and Community Service at Providence College. His current research concerns civic education, the political participation of young Americans, and the political representation of nonvoters. He has supervised hundreds of interns over the years. He holds a Ph.D. in political science from Rutgers University.

The Honorable Joan K. Christensen is a member of the New York State Assembly (119th District, Democrat). She has served as chair of the Legislative Women's Caucus (New York) and chair of the assembly's Task Force on Women's Issues. Prior to being elected to the state legislature, she served on the City of Syracuse Common Council and City of Syracuse Board of Assessment Review. Her assembly office has sponsored scores of interns over the years.

John "CZ" Czwartacki is director of the Public Affairs Division at the Federal Emergency Management Agency (FEMA) and adjunct instructor in the Communications Department of George Washington University. He is on leave from his position as partner at Greener and Hook, a communications firm in Washington, D.C. He previously served as press secretary and spokesperson for several members of Congress, including former Senate majority leader Trent Lott and the House Republican Conference. He also worked on the 1996 Dole-Kemp presidential campaign and served in the first Bush administration as a spokesperson for the Department of Housing and Urban Development.

Sandra L. Davis is executive assistant to the Honorable Joan K. Christensen. She is also a member of the Onondaga County Democratic Committee. She has served on the boards of directors of several nonprofit organizations. In addition, she is assistant editor of the *Annual Review of Sex Research* and a past managing editor of the *Journal of Sex Research*.

L. Elaine Halchin is an analyst in American national government at the Congressional Research Service. She specializes in the executive branch. Her publications have appeared in *The Good Society* and

School Choice in the Real World (book chapter). She holds a Ph.D. in political science from the Maxwell School of Citizenship and Public Affairs, Syracuse University.

Brett Heindl is a doctoral candidate in political science at the Maxwell School of Citizenship and Public Affairs, Syracuse University. A student of international relations and U.S. foreign policy, he has interned at the U.S. Department of State and the International Organization for Migration in Geneva, Switzerland.

Matthew Koch is currently serving in the Bush White House as the associate director of the Office of Cabinet Affairs. Prior to this he served in the Intergovernmental Affairs Office at the U.S. Department of Energy. During the Bush governorship, he was natural resource policy director for the Texas Office of State-Federal Relations in Washington, D.C. He has also been a district director and a legislative assistant for Congress, and a director of the Legislative Study Group for the New York State Assembly. In addition, he has experience directing political campaigns at the state, local, and federal levels.

R. Eric Petersen is an analyst in American national government at the Congressional Research Service. He has held several internships at the local, state, national, and international levels, including the Congressional Research Service. He holds a Ph.D. in political science from the Maxwell School of Citizenship and Public Affairs, Syracuse University, and an M.P.A. from Virginia Polytechnic Institute.

Ryan Petersen is assistant professor of political science at the College of the Redwoods. His research and teaching interests are in the areas of constitutional law, the U.S. Supreme Court, and American government. He is a Ph.D. candidate in political science at the Maxwell School of Citizenship and Public Affairs, Syracuse University.

Paul Scolese is an advisor in the Public Law and Policy Practice Group of Akin, Gump, Strauss, Hauer & Feld, L.L.P., in Washington, D.C.

Before joining Akin, Gump, he served in the Bush-Cheney presidential transition office as director of the Department of Commerce Advisory Committee. He has over ten years of Capitol Hill experience, most recently as staff on the House Commerce Committee. He holds an M.A. in history from Brown University.

Joanne Tait is executive coordinator and director of the intern program for the Sierra Club. She has also worked for Clean Water Action, based in Baltimore.

Jessica Wintringham is a Ph.D. student at the Maxwell School of Citizenship and Public Affairs, Syracuse University. She has served as deputy press secretary for U.S. Senator John Edwards and also worked in a similar capacity on his campaign. Her interests are in American politics, with a focus on gender and political participation.

First Words

Introduction

Grant Reeher and
Mack Mariani

In embarking on your political internship, you are beginning an experience that could literally change your life. Many public leaders were transformed by internship experiences during their college years: They evolved from someone interested in politics to someone for whom public service—either in elected politics or in some equally noteworthy capacity—is a calling and a lifelong career. Here is vice presidential candidate Senator Joseph Lieberman reflecting on his own undergraduate experience in his book, *In Praise of Public Life:*

> During the summer of 1963, I sought and received a student internship in Washington in the office of Connecticut's newly elected senator, Abe Ribicoff. To be in the capital city during the Kennedy administration, walking the streets and corridors of power, attending hearings and seeing the nation's leaders, was a thrill. But the opportunity to work for Ribicoff, to listen to him, watch him and learn from him, was truly a formative experience.

Of course, there are more "practical," even self-interested reasons for you to pursue and succeed in a political internship. Again, we will let the senator explain:

> Like any profession, getting in the door can be the hardest part. That's one of the primary values of an internship in any field—getting to know some of the people who are already in the profession you'd like to enter, let alone acquiring the specialized knowledge that defines that profession.

The fact that you are reading this book demonstrates that you understand the practical value of an internship. You are not alone. Indeed, every year literally thousands of you descend upon Washington, D.C., the fifty state capitals, and local political offices and organizations to volunteer your services as interns. A recent estimate published in an Associated Press news piece set just the D.C. figure at 65,000 interns per year. You bring with you intelligence, enthusiasm, and dedication, but precious little preparation. Unfortunately, you are rarely able to "hit the ground running."

Our guidebook is intended to help you make the most of your internship, both as a career prospect–enhancing experience and as a broader learning experience. We supply a set of practical, concise how-to essays written by political practitioners and by scholars with extensive experience supervising internships (most of the contributors are former interns themselves). Our book will be invaluable not only to you, the student intern, and your faculty supervisor but also, by extension, to the offices in which you work.

Our focus is the political internship—we are both political scientists, after all, and most of the internship experiences we supervise are politically oriented. Thus our book will help you to write good letters, conduct solid political research, interact with other members of the public and the media, and more generally make a positive contribution to the organization for which you are working. Perhaps the most useful chapter will be the final one, in which current undergraduates who have recently served as political interns tell you what to do and what not to do in order to succeed.

As you read, you will notice that we have included a lot of information that pertains directly to the Capitol Hill internship, which a large number of our students pursue; however, we also supply plenty of additional information on other kinds of political internships, including those at the White House, the bureaucracy, the Congressional district office, nonprofit organizations, and the state level. Furthermore, all of this material should prove extremely useful to students in a variety of other kinds of internships, both political and nonpolitical, national and local. This book will also be useful to students pursuing internships of different intensities and durations, from the part-time internships interwoven into an academic semester to full-time summer internships lasting anywhere from a few weeks to several months.

In the chapters to come you will encounter an abundance of useful specific advice. But let us begin this book with the most important overall pieces of advice, garnered from our collective experience of working with and supervising literally hundreds of interns.

First, remember that although you will most likely be working without being paid, you are nonetheless working. This is a job, probably your first "real" professional job. Do not make the mistake of thinking that because you are not being paid, you can show up and perform at your own convenience. In addition, do not make the mistake of thinking that because you are a student, the standards of responsible conduct to which you will be held in your internship are the same as those in effect at your college or university. Again, you are working now. Be a professional. The explanation that you couldn't perform your assignment because you felt a little under the weather, or because you were driving back home very late the night before, and so on, will not fly here. The internship you have is a precious placement; there are many other students who would like to trade places with you. Your organization is making an investment in you, in training you and in giving you the scarce resource of that cubicle or desk that you occupy. Despite making this fact clear to all of our students at the outset, we have nonetheless had the sad experience of finding out that a student has been "fired" from his or her internship. Don't let this happen to you.

Related to the fact that you are working in a real job is the additional fact that you are usually working for *someone*, rather than an organization. Everyone—you as an intern and the staff who supervise you—ultimately has the same boss, whether it's a member of Congress, a state legislator, an executive director of an interest group, or an agency head. One of us remembers the first day of his own first internship experience, in 1980 on Capitol Hill. Periodically, interspersed among all the phone calls handled individually and transferred electronically among different staffers in the office, someone would yell out, "It's the boss," and the person needed would immediately drop whatever he or she was doing and take the call, or run out the door. The first time this occurred, there was momentary confusion for this intern—why would Bruce Springsteen be calling here? But a second later it was clear. The mentality in most of the offices you will be working in will be closest, in this respect at least, to that of an entrepreneurial enterprise or small business. You are working for the business owner—and what he or she says goes. Thus, you'll notice that many of our chapter writers use that language, often referring to "the boss."

Second, in choosing your internship, try to pick something that relates to the issues and topics that most interest you. A student deeply interested in the environment might try to work for the Audubon Society or the Sierra Club, for instance. Do not, however, let your own political beliefs—what we political scientists like to call your ideology—overly constrict your possible choices. You are young! You are not sure entirely what you think, or at least you shouldn't be. Experiment. The best way to learn more about what you think and why you think it is to intimately explore different views. Many times the interns who have taken this advice have told us that the opportunity to learn about, and to learn from, a point of view they had previously disagreed with was the single most rewarding aspect of their experience.[1]

Third, if something is not going well, do not be afraid to take the initiative to change it. This means not simply complaining about spending eight hours a day at the copy machine, for instance, but rather proposing other ways in which you could better contribute to the organization, such as a specific significant project that you might complete. As we write this introduction, one of our students is in the middle of just such a process. Sofya Peysakhovich is a particularly conscientious student, intent on attending law school after she graduates, who is interning at a local district attorney's office. Though she has already had many great opportunities to observe what attorneys do and through that observation has learned a tremendous amount about criminal law, the kinds of tasks that she was given were mostly piecemeal and did not tax her intellectually. She approached her boss with an idea for a project that concerns police behavior, and the sometimes strained relations between students living off campus and the permanent residents who surround them. For her project she will collect data from police reports and then organize a panel discussion, open to both the university and the local community, that will be based in part on that data. Hers is the story of a good internship made much better through her own initiative.

Related to this point is the importance of persevering and of maintaining a good attitude while doing nonglamorous work. In most internships, there is a natural progression from starting at the most menial tasks to gradually working one's way up to do more interesting projects and activities—only if, that is, one does the initial tasks well and with a good attitude. Good things will come to you if you wait and then take the appropriate opportunities to make a positive proposal for putting more of your talents to use.

The office director at one of the local political internship placements where we send many of our students loves to tell the story of the intern who showed up for his first day of work and immediately asked where his own personal office was located and who would be his secretary. Needless to say, he did not get off to a good start.

Two additional points, related to each other: First, ask questions, both to learn more about politics and to find out how best to accomplish the task you've been assigned. But there are limits on how many questions you should ask and when you should ask them. Thus, you should read the chapters that follow carefully to get a clear sense of the best way to go about asking questions. Second, observe carefully what is going on around you, even when the tasks you are engaged in are menial. There are numerous examples sprinkled throughout these chapters of how interns learned interesting things in the most unexpected ways.

And finally, remember to work hard and have fun. State capitals and especially Washington, D.C., are wonderful places to be at any time of the year. There is always so much going on, politically and otherwise. So go to the political receptions. See the plays. Hear the concerts.

Regarding this final point, it is probably not too early to mention safety. Because of September 11, not to mention Chandra Levy's disappearance a few months before, potential interns and their parents are worried about safety. What we have to say here we believe to be common sense but nonetheless worth saying. Most political internships take place in large cities, such as Washington, D.C. Be careful. But keep in mind that you are in no more danger there than you would be in any other large city. Interns rarely have safety problems, and we believe that sensible students interning in large cities experience fewer problems, on average, than they do on their own campuses.

This book is divided into five parts. Part 1 includes this introduction and an essay by Joseph Cammarano, a colleague and good friend who has supervised hundreds of interns and is a leader in the service learning movement in higher education. He provides some "big picture" advice about the broader civic purposes of internships and explains what you should be getting out of the experience, as both a student and a citizen.

Let us add one thing to what he has to say in his essay. One of the most valuable gifts you may receive from your internship experience is a heightened and more nuanced understanding of politics and of politicians. It has been widely observed that we are living in a time of political cynicism and alienation. The data that illustrate this phenomenon are numerous and striking, but we will not try to relate them all here. As just one indicator, note that voting turnout is at an all-time low relative to our recent past—and even in the November elections immediately following September 11, when patriotism was sweeping the nation, turnout did not increase above recent levels for that kind of off-year election. Most worrisome is the fact that this sense of political alienation seems to be particularly concentrated among you, the nation's youth. Despite the fact that your generation is volunteering and engaging in "good works" at record-high levels, you remain alienated from politics and disconnected from political activity. To many of you, politics seems corrupt.

We believe that this attitude not only is debilitating to the health of our democratic process but is also misguided. Politics is better than that, as we hope your internship will demonstrate to you. Indeed, one of the most striking themes that comes back to us in the essays that our interns write at the completion of their service is embodied in the following example: "I never knew politicians worked so hard, and tried so hard to do the right thing. I'll never put them down again." Now, we don't want to excuse all politicians from the criticism that they may deserve, but we do hope your experience will provide you with an antidote to the knee-jerk disgust with political life that is currently infecting the nation.

Part 2 of the book contains chapters about different kinds of political internships. Although each chapter focuses on a specific political office, many of the chapters' lessons apply more broadly, so you should read through all of them regardless of your particular placement.

In the chapter on state legislative internships, for example, you learn the value of carrying a small notepad around with you at all times, to keep track of names, issues, procedures, and so on. We think this is essential advice for any intern. The same essay offers you the excellent advice that, if your internship is only part-time during the week, you should organize your time there in large blocks versus a few hours here and there; that way, you are more likely to get assigned more significant tasks. You also get wonderful advice about how to properly take a phone message—a skill more subtle, and more important, than it might at first appear—and a good tip about how to finish an internship so that you will be remembered fondly by your supervisor and the staff. In the chapter on the executive branch, you get great advice about the usefulness of observing how staffers interact with and lead others and about the value of appearing to be busy, even when you are not.

Part 3 contains chapters about conducting political research. Again, although much of this material is focused on the kinds of research that interns on Capitol Hill and elsewhere in Washington, D.C., most often engage in, it should be extremely useful to interns working in almost any political environment.

Part 4 concentrates on writing in the political environment, which is the task that interns often work up to after they have done their time at more mundane tasks. Again, these chapters are broadly applicable to most writing tasks. The authors include specific advice that extends beyond the particular task that concerns them. In the chapter on writing constituent letters, for example, there is an excellent suggestion about how to use a letter found while opening and reading the mail—a task interns learn to hate—in order to switch over to the more substantial and rewarding activity of crafting a response. And in the chapter on talking points and speeches, you learn about the importance of good timing in asking questions. Finally, though many of you will not be fortunate enough to actually engage in all the different kinds of writing that the chapters treat, reading all this material will provide you with helpful background knowledge about the way your office works.

In Part 5, former interns speak. In the fall of 2001, Grant Reeher conducted two lengthy focus groups at Syracuse University with sizeable groups of former interns, many of whom had logged two or more internship experiences. The remarks of these students were then edited to highlight the most important points and the most common themes. Here you will receive great advice about what to do, what not to do, what to seek, and what to avoid. The former interns also discuss how to avoid and, if necessary, respond to compromising personal situations.

As academics, the last thing we would want to do is denigrate the importance of the classroom. But we have found that the internship experience is often one of the most important experiences that our students have in their college years. We hope this book will help you make the most of that experience.

Go forth and conquer.

Note

1. If upon graduation you end up seeking full-time work in a partisan office, such as a congressional office on Capitol Hill or a party-based committee staff position, and you have a previous internship experience from the other side of the aisle, you may be questioned about this internship in your job interview. The explanation that you were interested in exploring different points of view and in keeping an open, less partisan mind while in college should be sufficient to allay anyone's concerns.

How to Read
Your Internship

Joseph Cammarano
PROVIDENCE COLLEGE

You are, no doubt, excited about your internship. Maybe you decided to study political science because you are interested in politics, and, as much as you may like (or dislike!) your classes, you've found they are often more talk than action. An internship allows you to jump into the trenches, get active, and work with other people who are committed to politics and political activism. Perhaps your internship is attractive because you have heard that a major in political science doesn't really prepare you for any kind of job, so the internship might give you practical experience that could help you get a job once you graduate. Maybe you are wondering whether all your coursework really relates to the day-to-day work of politics, and thus your internship will help you to gain a deeper understanding of the concepts and research that you read about and discuss in your classes. Whatever the reason, you have made a wise decision. Public service and political internships allow you to do all of these things.

My first internship helped me in two ways. First, I was always a political junkie, and working in politics gave me a sense of satisfaction that was missing from some of my courses. Second and perhaps more important, my internship helped to focus and energize my interest in political science. Observations and insights I gained in my internship helped me to make better course selections in subsequent semesters, gave me ideas for research paper

11

topics in my classes, and whetted my appetite for the type of research about politics that I still pursue today, nearly twenty years after the internship.

Just as you see an internship as a wonderful opportunity to broaden your knowledge, educators embrace internships because they enhance your education and provide you with unique learning opportunities. According to the National Society for Experiential Education learning from internships takes place in four areas. First, they allow you to apply the knowledge you have gained from studying politics to the workplace. This connects classroom learning to politics and allows the material you study to come alive. Second, you will gain knowledge about what people who are in public affairs or politics do, what skills or traits are needed, and whether you might want to pursue such careers when you complete your education. Third, internships help you acquire a set of skills that are in demand in any workplace. Finally, you will gain more confidence in yourself by developing your critical thinking skills and polishing your decision-making ability.

Rest assured that there will be countless learning opportunities during your internship, some of which will be obvious to you, others less so. For example, doing research for a local official on a public policy problem, helping to plan a political event, or sitting in on a staff meeting are all obvious learning opportunities. Almost any internship has such experiences. In such instances, you will find it easy to make connections between your work and studies. Working alongside political activists, you can see your studies come alive, and you can compare what you have learned to what is being done.

Keep in mind, however, that you are an *intern*, not a full-time employee. Interns are usually at the lower end of any organizational chart, and at times you will be asked to do things that seem to have little resemblance to learning about politics. After all, what can be learned from organizing files, answering phones, making photocopies, or doing other menial tasks? I hope to convince you that even these seemingly mundane tasks are important opportunities to gain new insights about politics. I recognize that this is a tough sell, but I am convinced I am right about this.

You also need to remember that you are a *student*, one who is doing an internship to get both work experience and to gain greater insights into your academic studies. Just as you read texts in classes, you need to view your internship site as a textbook. When you read the site as a text, be sure to read everything, critique the content of the site, and place the details of your experiences into broader concepts about politics.

There is a tendency to separate the study and the practice of politics. Your internship challenges such distinctions. Politics can teach us a great deal about political science, and political science can be of great use to those who participate in politics. So reject the idea that your studies have not prepared you for your internship and reject the notion that the only benefit you receive from an internship is work related.

In this chapter, I hope to help you to think about what it is you are learning from your internship, how to use your political science knowledge to inform your experience, and how to use your internship to inform your political science studies. First, I examine the obvious learning opportunities encountered during internships and make suggestions for enhancing the lessons gleaned from them. Second, I explore the question of what could possibly be learned from the menial tasks that are often part of an internship. Third, I address what questions to ask about your experiences so as to maximize your learning. Finally, I examine the big picture and try to assist you in seeing the connection between your internship and your political science education.

Making the Most of the Obvious Material

Of the hundreds of interns I have supervised, every one has at some point been given a meaningful, exciting, or fulfilling task to complete. Many students have had several such tasks in a single internship. There are countless examples of them, and you will no doubt know one when you have the experience. Here are some actual examples:

- Conducting research for a city council member on the effects of trash incinerators on surrounding neighborhoods
- Attending meetings of professional campaign staff to design an advertising campaign for a state legislative candidate
- Going to committee hearings and taking notes in order to assist a member of Congress in tracking issues
- Gathering information and creating a website for a state agency that lists grant opportunities for those interested in creating environmental education programs
- Working in a city mayor's office, coordinating special events, including visits of foreign dignitaries

In each of these experiences, the core duties of interns made it easy for them to understand the importance and relevance of their work to their studies. They completed tasks, interacted with political practitioners, observed politician-citizen contacts, conducted research, and participated in planning political events. All of these activities are easily linked to political science education. But do not simply accept these experiences at face value and assume that you are conscious of all the things you are learning. Digging deeper will broaden your knowledge of politics and give you a more sophisticated understanding of your internship experience.

To make this point more concrete, I highlight the internship experience of the student who worked in the mayor's office mentioned above. Karla entered the internship excited to have a position where she would be working closely with a popular and charismatic mayor.[1] At first she found the experience rewarding, solely because of the opportunity to help plan events and have frequent contact with the mayor. The mayor was jovial and seemed deeply committed to serving the people of the city, and the intern's greatest hopes were realized. The work she did on special events gave her practical experience in organizing, planning, and doing advance work. She met many of the people who comprise the local social, economic, and governing elite. Throughout the first portion of her internship she focused on these aspects of her learning.

As the internship progressed, however, Karla started to observe some patterns that led her to think more broadly about her experience. First, the mayor tended to make appearances only in the central business district and its immediate vicinity. Second, she noticed that the mayor treated staff very differently in private than when he was in public view. To put it politely, in his private behavior, the joviality of his public persona was nowhere to be seen. Third, she noticed that, despite the periodic abusive language used by the mayor in dealing with the professional staff, they were fiercely loyal, took the verbal abuse, and often defended this behind-the-scenes behavior as necessary venting for a person under great pressure.

By asking questions about these unsettling observations, Karla was able to connect each of them to her studies in political science. First, the bulk of appearances in the business district can be explained by the mayor's desire to keep in close contact with local elites, particularly those who contribute money to the mayor's reelection campaign and who make important decisions on locating jobs in the city. The second observation reminded the student of her studies in political psychology, particularly research on presidential character. She did some research into the mayor's background and developed her own assessment of his character. Third, the unbending loyalty of staff led Karla back to the literature on political patronage, which helped her understand that the mayor's staff received (and kept) their positions by virtue of their loyalty to the mayor, no matter how ill-mannered he may be in dealing with them. Most of the mayor's closest staff were early supporters of his political career and stuck with him through some troubling times. He in turn stuck by them. By the end of the semester, Karla had developed a clearer understanding of her experience, made a realistic assessment of the strengths and weaknesses of the mayor, and had a fuller, more complex understanding of political leadership.

Although Karla's deeper understanding came about as a result of negative observations, students have also deepened knowledge through observations of positive things. Kathryn, who interned in the district office of a member of Congress, observed an unusually large number of requests for assistance with the Immigration and Naturalization Service. Upon investigation, she discovered two important insights into the workings of the office. First, the representative had purposely hired experts in immigration policy to staff the district office because of the large proportion of first- and second-generation immigrants who resided in the district. Second, the representative had several family members and friends who were recent immigrants, and he felt a special dedication to assisting the needs of noncitizens. Both motivations are well addressed in political science literature on what motivates behavior of elected officials, and Kathryn left the internship with a greater admiration for both the political savvy and the personally rooted political commitment of the representative.

To make the most of those duties that are already gratifying, you need to engage in deeper reflection. The best way to do this is to ask questions. Who do you see in your work? Who *don't* you see, and why don't you see them? Why are you and the people around you doing *these* tasks? How did the people who work in your office get there? Why are they doing *this*, as opposed to something else? What is the *purpose* of these activities? Are political practitioners behaving in a manner consistent with what you have studied? What explains any differences between research and practice? These and other questions will assist you in digging beneath the surface of your experience, making connections between your academic studies and practical experience, and enhancing the learning that comes naturally from rewarding work experiences.

Reading Between the Lines

Long ago, a friend of mine named Glen, now a professor, worked as an intern in the national office of a major political party. The concept was a glamorous one. Working at the headquarters meant the intern had hit the big time, and this experience was sure to impress family, friends, and future employers. The romance soon faded, however, with the realization that the most important functions in this internship were clerical. Making photocopies, answering phones, running errands, and doing other mundane tasks quickly deflated the young intern's exaggerated sense of self-importance. The primary job responsibility seemed to be shielding party officials from anyone trying to speak directly to them, an unpleasant task, especially when there were repeat callers. After a few weeks of the internship, it became clear to Glen that the value of this experience was minimal at best and the learning from the job was apparently nonexistent.

But then something happened that changed Glen's mind. Every so often someone would place a call to the office and the staff would take it. Over time it became clear that some people were always put through while others were never put through, and the people who would get through were almost always calling from the White House, which was occupied at the time by a president from this political party. Why would party officials ignore calls from the offices of members of Congress, state party officials, the press, interest groups, and others yet take calls from seemingly unknown staffers in the White House?

Upon consultation with a professor, the answer became clearer. In studying the American presidency, Glen had learned about the many "hats" worn by the modern president. One of those hats is *party leader.* So the mystery was solved! Party officials took calls from the White House because, when those staffers call, they do so on behalf of the leader of their political party.

I share this story to illustrate how seemingly useless activities can be full of insights and opportunities to learn about politics. A rule of thumb about an internship is that there is almost always something to be learned if you think, observe, reflect, and connect experiences to your studies. Think about what it is you are doing. Resist the notion that it is the task alone that provides the lesson for you. For example, while interning at a political organization's office, Glen constantly had to do battle with a malfunctioning photocopy machine, which seemed to have been provided by the organization's political opponents as a means to distract them from their political activism. One day, out of frustration, he asked why they couldn't replace or at least properly repair the machine, so they could get documents copied and sent to the group's supporters. The response was that the organization could not afford a service contract, and so, when the machine broke, they had to try to fix it themselves. This seemingly mundane task quickly became a real-world lesson to the student on the disproportionate allocation of resources to political organizations. The other side had far greater financial resources (including *paid* internships) and so was surely able to have functioning photocopiers and who knows what else at their disposal to further their cause. That side won the next presidential election.

Other examples of common tasks given to interns that may seem at first like busywork but can deepen your understanding of politics include clipping newspaper articles, filing materials, sitting at a desk waiting for things to do, and writing form letters in response to constituent mail. There is some, though not much, value in learning the technical aspects of these tasks. But each one still provides you with learning opportunities beyond the simple accomplishment of the task. In clipping newspapers, you may notice patterns in the type of coverage your group or representative receives from the press, or you may notice that there is almost no coverage at all. You may realize that national issues receive far more coverage than local ones. By looking at this task more broadly, you can actually learn a great deal about press coverage of politics. In answering constituent mail, you can learn many things about the nature of demands placed on elected representatives, the types of problems people encounter with the bureaucracy, the degree to which letters are part of orchestrated campaigns by interest groups, and the retail nature of much of electoral politics.

Even simply sitting in an office, a seemingly passive and uninteresting activity for an eager intern, creates countless opportunities for students to use a method known as *participant observation* in studying the office in question. By watching who goes through the office and who doesn't, what is discussed and what is not discussed, and how people interact with each other, interns get a glimpse of political actors in their element. This can lead to many insights about how politics works, insights that cannot be effectively learned from reading a book. Sitting in an office for an extended period of time also gives interns the opportunity to engage in conversations with full-time staff and others who may come into the office. When lobbyists, citizens with needs or strong opinions on an issue, or the occasional sanity-challenged constituent enters an office, each provides an opportunity to learn. So, sitting in an office provides countless encounters with politics.

Despite the tendency for interns to focus on the obvious aspects of their work, my experience working with interns is that, with very rare exceptions, there is no such thing as a bad internship. All internships provide ample opportunities to learn, even those that have attached to them relatively mundane responsibilities. Again, looking beyond the tasks at hand to treat the internship site as a textbook, watching what is going on, trying to figure out why things work the way they do, and keeping an open mind will all help to enhance your learning.

Interrogating the Text

As I have made clear, the way to enrich your internship is to constantly ask questions. This is best done in some form of structured oral and written reflection. The way you do this depends upon the details of your internship. If it is tied to a course, your instructor will build into the course requirements ample opportunity to raise questions your work generates and to help relate internship experiences to your study of political science. If your internship is less structured, you alone will be responsible for raising questions to reflect upon. In either case, there are three venues where you should raise questions: on the job, with your faculty supervisor, and within yourself.

Interns are often reluctant to ask questions at their placement site. But questions are important, and they need to be asked so you can do your job effectively. Beyond those that help you understand how to do the nuts and bolts of your job, you should ask other questions as well. Why is the district office in its chosen location rather than somewhere else? What will be done with the database compiled during the internship? Why do campaigns have to ask for the occupations of major donors? Who determines the witnesses list and order of appearance at a committee hearing? The exact questions that come to you will vary with your knowledge and the details of your internship, and as they come, you need to ask them of the people at your site or jot them down for later. Of course, not every question should be asked, and you should be conscious of how sensitive your question is, but do ask questions. You'll be surprised at how open most people are to such inquiries, and you'll know immediately when you ask a question too sensitive to be answered (and that itself provides you with another learning opportunity).

The next series of questions you need to ask is of the instructor who is supervising your internship. If something you encounter makes no sense to you, or if it contradicts what you have studied in classes, bring this to your instructor's attention. If something you saw or did intrigues you, ask for additional information on it. In most cases, your instructor will already have supplied guiding questions, but do not let that constrain you from coming up with new ones.

Finally, you need to constantly ask questions of yourself. How do you like the experience? Does it meet your expectations or depart dramatically from them? What lessons have you learned? Do you enjoy politics more or less now that you are getting real-world experience? What kinds of careers related to your internship seem appealing to you? Again, individual experiences determine the questions to be asked, but asking them and developing some response to them is an important step in maximizing your learning.

Placing the Text in a Larger Context

To complete this discussion of what internships do for your education, I return to the issue first addressed in this chapter, the place of internships in undergraduate education, specifically in your study of the discipline of political science. Internships allow you to use your subject knowledge in an applied setting, to test your own interests and skills against potential careers, to acquire new skills, and to improve your self-confidence and decision-making abilities. In addition to these benefits, an internship will help you make better sense of your studies by giving you a chance to consider three issues. First, you can consider whether your experience confirms or refutes conventional wisdom about politics. Second, you can evaluate whether the research findings you study in your courses stand up to your field experience. Finally, internships help you think about larger theoretical issues relating to American democracy.

Testing Conventional Wisdom About Politics

There is a laundry list of words used to describe politics, politicians, and government. On the negative side, pick your adjective: greedy, corrupt, lazy, incompetent, two-faced, dishonest, selfish, or any of dozens of other criticisms hurled at politicians and public officials. This is the conventional wisdom presented on nearly any talk radio program and on most television programs. On the other side is the mythic ideal (personified by the likes of George Washington and Abraham Lincoln) often presented in elementary and high school civics books: the dutiful civil servant who pushes aside self-interest in pursuit of the public good, who does the right thing even in the face of harsh criticism.

Your internship should give you some basic insights into the accuracy of these stereotypes. Are public officials lazy and incompetent? Is the bureaucracy really as inefficient as popular critics claim? Is self-interest ever dismissed in favor of the public good? The odds are that your experience will suggest that nuance is more accurate than absolutes, and you will search for some middle ground that views politics as being about principle and public service but also recognizes that the actions of political actors are never far removed from self-interest.

Assuming you find that the people you work with are *neither* saintly nor sinister, you then need to assess why popular sentiment is often expressed through these simplistic stereotypes. Why do people think the way they do about politics and politicians? Did you encounter something in your internship that helps to identify and explain some of the sources of these stereotypes? Stereotypes have their sources in both rhetorical argument and in empirical observation. Consider the aspects of the organizations and the people you worked with that might feed into cultural depiction of politics and politicians. Also, consider the implications of such stereotypes for politics. Do prevailing cultural stereotypes of politics deter people (including you) from being active? How does what you've observed compare with media portrayals?

There are many related questions to be asked about how realistic popular wisdom is about politics. Given your exposure to such descriptions, your studies in political science, and your internship experience, you are in a unique position to develop a more complex, more complete understanding of how politics works. Be sure to do so.

Weighing the Usefulness of Political Science Research

In addition to weighing the evidence regarding how politics is depicted in our culture, there is an equally valuable educational benefit of internships: They serve as a field test for your studies. At times, the academic study of politics may seem to relate to anything *but* the real world, but in fact the expressed goal of the field of political science is to systematically study, analyze, and theorize about politics. So you should have a great deal of knowledge about politics going into your internship. In some cases, the utility of your political science knowledge will be obvious (for example, in understanding how to do research or knowing legislative processes). Other times, the connection between political science and internships occurs over time, as comparison between knowledge and experience results in what some call the *aha! moment*, a revelation of how things fit together. In any case, an internship is both informed by and informative for academic study.

In assessing the links between education and practice, you need to consider how your studies apply to your work setting. Do the theories and concepts covered in courses manifest themselves in your setting? If your internship is legislative, you may wish to consider whether ambition theory, the notion that politicians act in predictable ways to maximize advancement and minimize risk of loss, explains the behavior of the politicians you encounter. If your internship relates to political communication, you can evaluate the literature on agenda setting. If the internship is in the bureaucracy, assess how the agency balances the demands of the principals (the executive and legislative branches and interest groups) with obligations to implement laws fairly and without prejudice. If the internship is judicial, evaluate how research on plea-bargaining and prosecutorial discretion helps to explain the outcomes of cases. The precise way you weigh your political science knowledge against practice depends on the circumstances of the internship and your own knowledge of the field. Rest assured, though, that, so long as you have had at least an introductory politics course, there are ample opportunities for you to compare research with practice.

Another way that internships can enhance your academic knowledge arises when there are competing theories about political behavior, institutions, and processes. Although internships must not be used to generalize to all similar experiences, they can serve as a baseline in comparing the relative merits of academic arguments about the same phenomena. One example here is taken from the earlier discussion of the student who interned with the mayor's office. At the end of the semester, this student was able to assess the relative merits and weaknesses of elitist and pluralist theories and draw some conclusions about who really governs the city.

Another example of how internships can assist in comparing various theories about politics comes from a student who worked on a political campaign. Over the course of the campaign, the student was confronted with two seemingly contradictory realities. On one hand, the campaign itself conformed to the *candidate-centered* model, in that the candidate was a self-starter, had created a separate organization, raised lots of money, and hired political consultants to craft and implement campaign plans. On the other hand, as the campaign progressed, the student discovered that much of the money raised was done so with direct assistance from the national and local political party organizations and that desperately needed money from the party (so-called *coordinated expenditures*) was promised only after the candidate took specific issue positions and hired consultants whom were satisfactory to party officials. The experience led the student to understand that, despite the candidate-centered perspective's substantial merit, there are reasons to believe that political parties exert far more influence than is immediately evident. The experience also helped the student to consider the complex dynamics involved in campaign politics, a complexity cited often in the political science literature.

Evaluating Democratic Theory and Practice

The final value of internships to higher education lies in the opportunities they provide to link practical experience to normative (value-oriented) considerations of politics. They are important for encouraging us to assess the quality of our political system and how well it lives up to the principles of democracy. They force us to face both the good and bad aspects of our republic and to consider reforms necessary for improving our political system.

In your internship you will have the opportunity to see how politics works. You will observe citizens and public officials engaging in political persuasion. You will witness political processes and deal with the consequences of decisions made by those in authority. In addition to learning about the mechanics, you also need to consider the larger issues that emerge. Is everyone treated equally? Does everyone have genuine access to governance? Which biases are obvious, and which are less so? Has our system adapted well to the dramatic changes that have occurred in the world, or have we strayed too far from the founding design? Is the contemporary reality of politics one that is responsive and accountable to citizens? These and many other questions may emerge from your experience. To realize the educational objectives of internships fully, you must wrestle with larger issues, ask tough questions about the people you encounter, and make judgments about whether things work as they should.

I often instruct our students about to start internships to first read or reread James Madison's *Federalist* No. 10. It is probably the best single preparation for making sense of the various experiences one will have in an internship, and it provides a framework for addressing issues of American democracy. In this document, Madison lays out the basic assumptions of human nature (we can't help it—

we are all self-interested), the consequences of these assumptions (we will organize with others who have similar interests to get what we want and will seek to impose our interests on others), and the virtues of the Constitution in dealing with the realities of human nature and the emergence of such interest groups (a large republic governed by a diverse body of representatives rather than a small republic governed by democratic impulses). At the end of the internship experience, I ask students to return to the document and assess the degree to which Madison's theory describes contemporary politics and to consider whether the Madisonian answer to the problems of democracy and faction are a source of strength in our political system or a sign of major weakness. This consideration of Madison will ultimately lead to a broader examination of politics, deeper reflection on the virtues and the consequences of our political system, and an appreciation for the dynamics of politics as it is practiced in the United States.

I recommend *Federalist* No. 10 to you as a way to move from direct experience to conceptual analysis. But whether or not you use James Madison to engage in an evaluation of democracy, this evaluation is in many ways the most important learning task for you, so do not neglect it.

The Final Exam

There is an educational reason for including internships as part of your academic studies. Liberal arts educators seek to develop the overall intellectual formation of students, to impart knowledge of substantive content, to foster analytical and critical thinking skills, and to give students transferable skills that will serve them well no matter what career path they choose. Internships assist in the achievement of these goals by sending students out into the political world to apply existing knowledge, to hone basic skills, to broaden their experience, and to learn more about the application of core concepts. So although you may look upon your internship as a chance to get off campus, do something tangible with your time, and be part of the excitement that surrounds public service, it is much more than that. It is an integral part of your education. Be sure to treat it as such. And don't stop observing, asking questions, and culling lessons from the obvious and the not-so-obvious job activities. And one last reminder: use the site as a textbook. Your internship site is a comprehensive source of information and—just like regular texts—must be read, studied, discussed, and written about if you are to learn the most you can from it.

Note

1. *Karla* is a pseudonym.

Basic Rules to Live By

3

The Capitol Hill Internship

Paul Scolese
AKIN, GUMP, STRAUSS, HAUER & FELD, L.L.P.

and *Mack Mariani*
SYRACUSE UNIVERSITY

One of the first things you will notice about interning in a congressional office is that, for the most part, the legislative branch of our nation's government is run by people in their twenties and thirties who are barely out of college or graduate school. Many of these staff members got their start sitting where you are—at an intern's desk, answering phones, opening mail, and helping with administrative duties in the office.

If you are like most interns, you will feel a bit overwhelmed your first week on the job. Your intern area will be cramped and uncomfortable. You may get little work the first few days. Staff members might walk right by you in a flurry of activity without even acknowledging your presence. You may find yourself sitting in a packed congressional cafeteria, eating lunch by yourself, wondering whether you have what it takes to succeed in the "big leagues" of national politics. Don't worry. Most congressional interns feel exactly the same way (the authors of this chapter certainly did). Your intern area may always be uncomfortable, but the staff members will learn your name, there will be work to do (a lot of it), and you won't have to eat lunch by yourself (unless you want to).

Although you are starting at the bottom, you have a great learning opportunity in front of you. You will learn firsthand how the legislative process works, and you will get the opportunity to learn what it means to be a professional in a highly competitive field. You may also build a strong foundation for your own career, whether it is in politics, law, academia, or some other field. Regardless of where you go from here, the lessons you learn in your congressional internship are sure to be lasting ones—so be sure to soak them in.

There are three distinct types of congressional internships: an internship in a member of Congress' personal office, in a congressional committee, and in a congressional leadership office. Since most congressional internships take place in members' personal offices, we will focus a great deal on those internships. In addition, we will briefly examine the committee offices and leadership offices to consider the role interns play in those settings as well.

Personal Offices

Every member of Congress operates a personal office on Capitol Hill that enables him or her to carry out the duties of a representative. This office is in addition to the one the representative operates back home in the state or congressional district he or she represents. There are 540 personal offices—one for every senator, house member, and delegate to Congress. Because there are so many of them, the vast majority of congressional interns will work in one of these personal offices. (See MAP 3.1.)

Members' personal offices are located in one of six principal office buildings opposite the Capitol along Independence Avenue (for the House) and Constitution Avenue (for the Senate). House members' personal offices are located in the Cannon, Longworth, and Rayburn House Office Buildings along Independence Avenue. Personal offices for U.S. senators are located in the Russell, Hart, and Dirksen Senate Office Buildings along Constitution Avenue.

Each member of the House of Representatives receives funding to hire as many as eighteen full-time and two part-time staffers. In contrast, senators receive their funding based on the population in

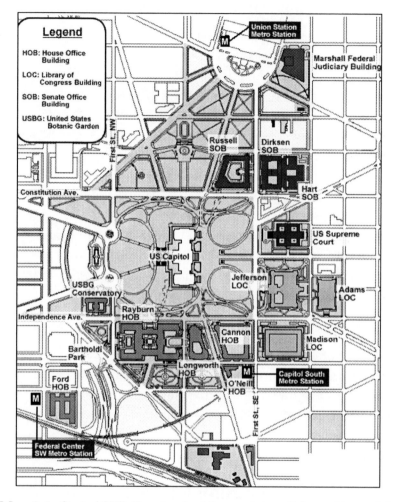

Map 3.1: *Capitol Hill. Reprinted with permission of the architect of the Capitol.*

their home state. Thus the number of staff members for each senator varies, sometimes widely. Members of the House and Senate must decide how to distribute their limited staff resources between their Washington and district offices—a task made somewhat simpler by the limited amount of space most of them have in their Capitol Hill offices.

Members of Congress are free to organize their offices as they choose, but most offices follow a similar structure:

The Administrative Assistant (AA)

The top staff member for a member of Congress is referred to as the administrative assistant (AA), or sometimes as the chief of staff. In most of corporate America, an administrative assistant is a personal secretary. In congressional offices, however, the administrative assistant is the most powerful staff member in the office. The AA is responsible for all the office's operations and serves as a top advisor to the member on both policy and political issues. Although the AA rarely supervises interns directly, he or she may ask you for administrative help, delivering a message, making photocopies, or walking a letter over to another office.

Although some members choose to have their AA or chief of staff work out of the congressional district offices, in most cases he or she will work out of the Washington office and a district director will be in charge of running the offices back home.

The Scheduler

Members of Congress typically have a scheduler, personal assistant, or office manager who is responsible for organizing their meetings, arranging their travel, and sorting through a multitude of invitations and meeting requests from constituents, government officials, and interest groups. In some cases, staff members in these positions will also have responsibility for general office administration, managing the paperwork and attending to the human resource needs of the office. Some offices will have more than one individual handling these duties, with at least one person in the district offices and one or more in the Capitol Hill office. Senators may have staff members in all three positions and typically have more than one scheduler. Interns often help the scheduler by making phone calls to confirm or reschedule meetings, greeting visitors in the office, or sending form letters to respond to invitations made by constituents or interest groups.

The Press Secretary

Members of Congress also employ a press secretary or communications director to manage media relations for the office. A House member typically has one staff member handling media relations. In contrast, a senator might have an entire press office, with a communications director overseeing the work of several press secretaries. In either case, a press secretary's responsibilities include writing press releases, speeches, and statements, as well as coordinating interviews, press conferences, and media opportunities. Usually, the press secretary is also responsible for monitoring the national and local media to ensure that the legislator and key staff members are kept up-to-date on local and national issues. Interns may accompany the press secretary to media events, help set up a press conference, or distribute a press release to members of the media. Interns are usually responsible for maintaining a media file for the congressional office, and the press secretary oversees their work of copying, distributing, and filing news articles of interest from local or national papers.

The Legislative Director (LD)

The legislative director (LD) manages the legislative functions of a congressional office; crafting and implementing the member's legislative agenda and strategy and advising him or her on floor and committee votes. In most offices, the legislative director also oversees the constituent mail program. The LD supervises a staff with one or more legislative assistants and possibly one or more legislative correspondents. Together, the legislative director and the legislative assistants and correspondents constitute a congressional office's "legislative staff." As an intern, you may be asked by the legislative director to conduct basic legislative research, write a response to a constituent letter, or provide other administrative support for the legislative staff.

Legislative Assistants (LAs) and Legislative Correspondents (LCs)

Legislative assistants (LAs) are responsible for working with the legislative director to coordinate the member's legislative agenda, monitor floor and committee votes, meet with constituents and lobbyists regarding legislation, and brief the member on legislative issues. Each LA covers a number of different issue areas (one LA covers

health and human services, science and technology, and veterans issues, while another covers tax, budget, and defense issues, and so on).
On the House side, most LAs are responsible for writing responses
to constituent letters pertaining to their issue areas. In some cases, an
office will have one or more legislative correspondents (LCs), whose
job it is to write constituent response letters, freeing LAs for more
substantive legislative work. Because Senate staffs are larger and
there are added resources for additional LAs and LCs, the typical
Senate LA can focus on a smaller number of issues.

Interns often assist LAs with constituent correspondence and
legislative research as well as general administrative tasks like
photocopying or mailing out form letters. Make no mistake, LAs
are the workhorses in a congressional office. They do most of the
research and letter writing and are the experts in their office on
the issues facing Congress in their legislative areas. For this reason, building a good working relationship with an LA is probably
the best way for an intern to get more substantive work.

Staff Assistants

Staff assistants perform entry-level administrative work in a congressional office. This includes greeting visitors, opening and distributing mail, answering phones, arranging White House or Capitol tours
for visiting constituents, processing requests for flags flown over the
U.S. Capitol, filing paperwork, and doing other administrative duties. Interns assist staff assistants by answering phones, greeting visitors, and processing tour and flag requests.

Committee Offices

One of the principal ways Congress manages its tremendous workload is by dividing its work among approximately two hundred
congressional committees and subcommittees.[1] The committee
system enables a smaller group of members to focus in greater detail on a piece of legislation or a set of related issues. Many members of Congress sit on more than one committee and serve on a
number of subcommittees.

Standing, Joint and Select Committees

Each chamber establishes its own standing committees at the beginning of each Congress. These standing committees are responsible for legislation and issues related to a specific subject area, as well as oversight over one or more executive branch agencies. The House of Representatives has twenty standing committees and the Senate has sixteen (see Box 3.1).

From time to time, the House and Senate also create select committees to study specific issues, conduct investigations, or consider legislation on matters of particular importance. While House and Senate committee systems are generally separate, Congress has created several joint committees. While joint committees do not handle legislation, they can hold hearings and issue studies. In addition, joint committees are often responsible for internal management tasks pertaining to both chambers.[2]

Box 3.1 Standing committees of the House and Senate.

House Standing Committees

Agriculture; Appropriations; Armed Services; Budget; Education and the Workforce; Energy and Commerce; Financial Services; Government Reform; House Administration; International Relations; Judiciary; Resources; Rules; Science; Small Business; Standards of Official Conduct (Ethics); Transportation and Infrastructure; Veterans Affairs; Ways and Means.

Senate Standing Committees

Agriculture, Appropriations; Armed Services; Banking, Housing and Urban Affairs; Budget; Commerce, Science, and Transportation; Energy and Natural Resources; Environment and Public Works; Finance; Foreign Relations; Governmental Affairs; Health, Education, Labor, and Pensions; Judiciary; Nutrition and Forestry; Rules and Administration; Small Business; Veterans' Affairs.

How Committees Operate

The rules of the House and Senate outline the duties, powers, responsibilities, and jurisdictions of each committee. Although each committee may organize differently, there are some basic characteristics that most of them share.

The principal way committees gather information is by conducting hearings. Hearings give committee members the opportunity to hear from government officials, outside experts, interest groups, and citizens regarding an issue, an agency, or a piece of legislation. Committees with authority over legislation can also alter—or "mark up"—a piece of legislation before voting on it. In most cases, legislation has first to be approved by a committee before the full House or Senate can consider it. The work of a committee is often

---

Box 3.2   Selected party leadership positions in the House and Senate.

House

Speaker of the House

Majority Leader

Minority Leader

Majority Whip

Minority Whip

House Republican Conference Chair

House Republican Policy Committee Chair

House Democratic Caucus, Chair and Vice Chair

Senate

Majority Leader

Minority Leader

Assistant Majority Leader (Majority Whip)

Assistant Minority Leader (Minority Whip)

Democratic Policy Committee Chair

Senate Republican Conference Chair

Senate Republican Policy Committee Chair

divided among various subcommittees that focus on a handful of issues under the full committee's jurisdiction. These subcommittees hold hearings on policy issues or conduct oversight and investigation of a particular government program or agency.

In many committees, the chair of the full committee sets the committee's agenda. He or she determines what hearings will be held, what agencies or programs will be investigated, and what legislation will be considered in committee. Subcommittee chairs are given varying amounts of leeway to address policy issues of interest to them, provided that they assist the chair in moving his or her policy agenda forward.

Committee Staff

Each committee has a staff, whose function is to assist the committee in carrying out its legislative and oversight responsibilities. In some committees the chair of the full committee hires all staff (including subcommittee staff or committee staff assigned to handle subcommittee issues), while in others, each subcommittee chair is allowed to hire a limited number of staff to work directly for the subcommittee.

The committee staff generally include:

- A *chief of staff* or *staff director*, responsible for managing the committee and serving as the chief policy and political advisor to the committee chair.
- A *chief counsel* or *general counsel*, an attorney responsible for the committee's legislative, oversight, and investigative activities.
- A *parliamentarian*, who handles the committee's procedural and jurisdictional activities and assists the chief counsel.
- One or more *counsel*, attorneys assigned to specific policy or oversight issues. Counsel are responsible for arranging and staffing hearings, drafting legislation, conducting legislative negotiations, and providing other legal assistance to the committee.
- A number of *clerks*, who assist counsel and provide specialized services such as recording committee votes, compiling and

preparing legislation for floor consideration, and putting together committee reports and other committee documents.

- *Professional staff members*, nonattorneys who are often experts in policy areas under the jurisdiction of the committee. They generally carry out many of the same functions as the committee counsel, helping draft and negotiate legislation and working with outside groups, members of Congress, and executive branch officials on issues before the committee.
- An *office manager*, in charge of the committee's administrative operations and offices.
- *Staff assistants*, who perform the general administrative duties in the office, such as receiving visitors, answering phones, making copies, setting up the committee room, and filing paperwork.
- *Interns*, who help staff assistants perform administrative tasks, including opening the mail, answering phones, and making copies. As an intern, you might also be asked to assist counsel or professional staff members with legislative or legal research. Unlike work in personal offices, which centers on constituent service, congressional committee work focuses mainly on the substantive legislative issues under the committee's jurisdiction. There will be little, if any, constituent mail to answer. Because committee work is specialized, the interns who secure these positions often have an interest in or a background related to the committee's work.

Leadership Offices

Political parties in Congress play a key role in organizing the workload and structuring the decision-making process. The role of parties has been institutionalized in Congress's decision-making process. Republican members of Congress make up the House Republican Conference and Senate Republican Conference in their respective chambers. The Democrats in Congress are organized similarly, into the House Democratic Caucus and Senate Democratic

Caucus. Party members from each chamber elect their own leadership, whose job it is to organize, promote, and implement their party's agenda. (See Box 3.2.)

Leadership offices receive taxpayer funding, including funding for staff. Unlike a personal office, whose main attention is on the constituency in the district, leadership offices focus on maintaining the support of a very particular constituency: the members of the party caucus or conference that elected them. Leadership offices are headed by a chief of staff (the title *administrative assistant* is generally used only with personal offices). Legislative and policy operations are run by a policy director; media operations are handled by a press secretary or communications director.

There are relatively few interns who work in leadership offices. This is true for three reasons: first, compared with the number of personal offices, there are only a few leadership offices. Second, many leadership offices are located in the U.S. Capitol itself, rather than the surrounding House or Senate office buildings. The positions are therefore prestigious, but the price for that prestige is office space that is relatively small and cramped. As a result, there is little room for staff, not to mention interns. Third, leadership offices are politically sensitive operations, where important political strategies are first developed and last-minute deals are finally struck. As a result, leadership offices often look for interns who have demonstrated their loyalty to the party, usually by participating in party activities at the local or college level.

Nonetheless, leadership offices—like other congressional offices—do rely on support from interns. Though leadership internships can be more difficult to obtain, they can be very exciting, offering interns an up-close look at the way political parties and their leaders operate on Capitol Hill.

Expectations for Interns

Provide Administrative Support

As an intern you should not expect to write speeches, draft legislation, or make major policy decisions for the member of Congress. You should expect to do a lot of clerical and administrative support work. Most likely, you will spend most of your time opening and sorting mail, answering phones, and making copies. Don't get disappointed. Remember: everybody has to start somewhere. If you do a good job and have a good attitude, you will get the chance for more substantive work, like conducting research or writing constituent letters. Keep in mind, though, that your first role is administrative support. Any substantive work you do will be *in addition to* your administrative responsibilities. Your substantive assignments will quickly disappear if you let your main responsibilities slide.

Act like a Professional

The job interns perform on Capitol Hill is essential. In most cases, you will be treated like a member of the staff—even if you aren't paid. In return, however, you are expected to treat your internship like a job. The basic expectations are obvious: get to work on time, don't leave early, follow through on your assignments, and dress appropriately for the office environment. Beyond that, be sure to avoid the obvious screwups that are all too commonplace but easily avoided. Don't make personal long-distance phone calls from the office or spend most of your day on the Internet. Every office has a "disaster intern" story—like the intern we know who thought it was acceptable to wear shorts to work or the one who thought it was okay to drink a few beers with his lunch. Don't let that be you.

Use Discretion

As a general rule, you should not discuss office business with people outside the office. As an intern you will be exposed to political and policy discussions of a sensitive nature, and you may be exposed to details about the personal lives of the legislators and staff. These details, whether personal or political, should remain in the office. Remember: Capitol Hill is a very small community where it seems as if everyone knows one another. If you discuss sensitive office matters over dinner with friends, odds are that someone at your table or within earshot of your conversation will repeat it. This kind of gossip can unfairly hurt reputations, undermine office morale, and jeopardize careers (namely, yours).

Maintain a Positive Attitude

Internship positions are highly sought after; in fact, most members of Congress turn away at least as many interns as they accept. You should appreciate the opportunity that you have and make the most of it. Besides, you haven't earned the right to complain yet. As an intern, you have a relatively low-stress job. You don't work the long hours that the staff does—and even if you do, it is only for the duration of your internship. If you can't perform your internship duties without maintaining a positive attitude, the staff will quickly lose confidence in your ability to do more substantive work.

Suggestions for a Positive Internship Experience

Set Realistic Expectations and Share Them with Your Supervisor

Although your role as an intern will be primarily administrative, you may reasonably expect to get the chance, at some point in your internship, to tackle more substantive work. It makes sense to sit down with your supervisor at the beginning of your internship and discuss your expectations as well as what the office expects from you. Make your expectations reasonable. Although you probably won't write a speech for the member of Congress, you could get the chance to conduct legislative research for the staff, help draft talking points for a meeting with constituents, or write a constituent response letter. Share these expectations with your supervisor early on and revisit them after you have had a few weeks to settle into your position. If you are fulfilling your responsibilities as an intern, your supervisor should make sure that the office fulfills its responsibility to make your internship a rewarding and educational experience.

Get Out of the Office

Many of the best learning experiences for you will take place outside your congressional office. Work with your supervisor to make sure you go to a committee hearing or committee markup with your member of Congress. If that can't be arranged, find another committee meeting that interests you (check *Congress Daily*) and go sit in the audience. Ask for an afternoon off and spend some time in the House or Senate gallery watching a floor debate. Schedule these activities in advance with your supervisor so they don't interfere with your work responsibilities. Although you can watch congressional debates live on C-Span or C-Span 2, there is something special about being there in person.

Do the Little Things Right

The staff will take note of your ability to handle the simple, everyday, mundane tasks, like making copies and greeting visitors. If you bungle these simple jobs or if you have a negative attitude about them, you will be less likely to be assigned more challenging (and interesting) work. If you take pride in the details of your work and follow through on your assignments, the staff will look to you for help when more important projects come along.

One area that seems to cause interns a lot of trouble is phone messages. When taking a message, take the time to do it right. Get the caller's first *and* last name. Get a phone number where he or she can be reached. Ask what the call is regarding. And make sure to deliver the message as promptly as possible. Failing to do the little things right—like taking a phone message—can undermine your hard-earned reputation as a reliable intern.

Volunteer

When you are done with your work, ask for more. Don't sit around if there is work to be done. Volunteer for everything, even the most mundane tasks—it shows your enthusiasm and demonstrates that you are a team player. After you have established yourself, ask your supervisor if you can sit in on a meeting or write a constituent letter. Staff members in a congressional office have a lot of work to do, so they may not take the time to find you good projects unless you ask for them.

Read What the Staff Reads

Most congressional aides are addicted to news—they read everything—including no less than four daily newspapers (the *Washington*

Post, Wall Street Journal, New York Times, and *Washington Times*), a daily news subscription service called *The Hotline,* and two twice-weekly newspapers covering Capitol Hill—*Roll Call* and *The Hill.* If you want to understand what is going on both inside and outside your office, you should keep up with current events. Of course, you should make sure it doesn't interfere with your work. Read the paper on your lunch hour or come in a few minutes early.

Our final advice is to have fun. Congressional internships are hard work, but they should be fun too! For most interns, living in Washington, D.C., is a once-in-a-lifetime experience. Take time out to see the sights. Go to the Smithsonian; walk the mall; visit the White House. The nation's capitol is a great place to work and play; be sure to take time out to be a tourist while you're there. And take pictures—you will appreciate it later!

Notes

1. Carol Hardy Vincent, "Committee Types and Roles," *Congressional Research Service Report for Congress,* March 11, 1998.
   2. Ibid.

4

The District Office Internship

Matthew Koch
ASSOCIATE DIRECTOR, OFFICE OF
CABINET AFFAIRS, THE WHITE HOUSE

All politics is local.
—FORMER HOUSE SPEAKER
THOMAS P. "TIP" O'NEILL, JR.

District office workers are the front lines for members of Congress, state legislators, and other elected officials. Their job is crucial. They are the primary points of contact for most of the legislators' constituents, opinion leaders, local elected and party officials, and major donors. Consider the case of a member of the U.S. House of Representatives. To meet with every constituent he or she represents, a member of Congress would have to talk to almost six thousand constituents every week of the office's two-year term. A good district office operation is the key to reelection and a long, successful political career. Despite members' importance and power in Washington, if their district office cannot provide good constituent service, they will be looking for a new job after the next election.

Keep in mind that as an intern in a district office you will rarely get to rub elbows with national political figures, write legislation, or attend a policy briefing. Even so, the most fundamental work and duties of representative government and its services are performed in district offices. A district office internship will give you the chance to learn a great deal about government and local politics, and you can apply the lessons you learn in a district office to any level of government.

As an intern, you should expect to spend a lot of time making copies, filing paperwork, and answering telephones. Everyone in the office performs these tasks. If you show that you are capable of performing the most mundane jobs with interest and professionalism, you will soon be given more challenging and interesting work to do.

Don't expect to be writing or giving speeches, briefing the Congress member on policy, or drafting position papers. In a congressional office, it is recognized that these jobs require specific skills and experience. You can more realistically expect to assist with researching policy positions, locate information, and accumulate material for speeches, briefs, and position papers.

Although I was never an intern myself, I have seen firsthand how important internship experience can be. An internship will help you prepare for the demands of a career in politics. It will help you focus on the things you like to do and steer you toward the jobs you find most gratifying. I've worked in many facets of government and politics—on Capitol Hill; in a Congressional district office; in a state legislature; in federal, state, and local campaigns; on a governor's staff; and now in a presidential administration. I have hired former interns and referred them to open positions, and I have seen them succeed as campaign managers, district directors, press secretaries, lobbyists, and White House staffers. A few have even become elected officials themselves. Even if you don't choose a career in politics, understand that your political internship will provide you with unique insights into a segment of our culture that affects you and every aspect of our society.

The "Typical" District Office

Congressional staffs vary in size and are limited to approximately seventeen employees for the Washington and district offices combined. When you consider that a district for a member of the U.S.

House of Representatives has almost 600,000 people, seventeen employees is a relatively small number and a main reason that the staff rely on the help of interns. Each senator represents an entire state and staffs approximately forty employees in all his or her offices combined.

House members' district office operations typically have from six to ten employees. Working with so few staff, you will have the opportunity to do a variety of tasks, if you are capable and show an interest. Most district offices have employees performing similar jobs and duties, often with similar titles.

The District Director

The district director is responsible for managing the office and the district staff. He or she oversees all the work in the district office and, of all the district staff, has the most daily interaction with the elected official. The district director is usually accountable only to the representative or senator and the chief of staff. At times this function is filled by the chief of staff.

In addition to managing the staff and the day-to-day operations of the district office, the district director represents the senator or representative at meetings or events. He or she is responsible for developing and maintaining relationships with local government officials, political party leaders, and major campaign supporters and is the office's principal point of contact for important visitors. The director often manages special projects, which may vary from overseeing the writing, production, and mailing of a special newsletter to a major request from a local municipality for special assistance from the federal government.

The district director's job requires political savvy, knowledge of how the federal government operates, appreciation for the importance of constituent service and the willingness to achieve it, and the ability to manage staff and the day-to-day operations of a congressional office. Most important, he or she must understand and be effective in guiding the office toward the ultimate goal of getting the representative or senator reelected. The successful district director must have an understanding of the "big picture"—pay close attention to how the staff work and keep them moving forward to Election Day.

Although your interaction with the district director may be limited, you would be wise to closely observe how he or she manages the office and staff. Also, be cognizant that the district director is more aware of your work and your role in the office than you may think. Keeping the "office machine" and all of its parts functioning well is the director's job.

The Press Secretary

District offices may have a press secretary. A district press secretary's duties include responding to local press queries, being a spokesperson for the member of Congress to the local media, and—most important—generating as many positive media stories for the member as possible. He or she must also coordinate press conferences for the member. A press secretary promotes, sells, protects, and manages the elected official's public image. In addition, a press secretary is responsible for writing other materials for publication, including press releases, opinion editorials (op-eds), newsletters, and other forms of direct mail. A press secretary may work out of the district or Washington office; some members have a press secretary in both offices.

Press secretaries must be swift thinkers who can respond quickly and appropriately to questions from the press with the right comment or quote. They also need to have the ability to write accurately under deadline and to sell a story—quickly generating press releases in reaction to events with the hope of generating positive media coverage for their boss. They must develop or have relationships with the local media—which can help get an important quote or story placed in a newspaper or on television, or assist with having a damaging quote or story removed or withheld from publication. Other duties may include providing the Washington office with daily news clips on national and district current events and maintaining files of news stories about the member of Congress. A press secretary must also monitor the local media coverage for stories on the member.

An intern can provide great assistance to a press secretary. When he or she is under deadline, you may be able to help the press secretary by faxing out press releases or assisting at press conferences. You can also expect to help with copying and faxing daily news clips to the Washington office and with monitoring the local print and electronic (television and radio) news coverage.

Observe how the press secretary speaks to the press, how she plans a media "strategy," her writing style, what she considers media "opportunities," and what daily press stories she feels are important to the representative or senator.

The Scheduler

A Congress member's scheduler is another position that may be located in the Washington or district office, or both. This person must keep track of and respond to all requests for meetings and appearances and properly coordinate the member's schedule. It is often a difficult and sometimes thankless job. The good ones are invaluable and in high demand.

The scheduler's job demands incredible organizational skills. A scheduler must be able to organize the boss's workday, political schedule, and personal time effectively and efficiently and manage an ever changing schedule. He or she needs to judge which requests for meetings or events are priorities based on the nature of the meeting and who is requesting the meeting. He or she must know how to properly and graciously respond to invitations. A scheduler must also be able to find events or create meetings to fill up a schedule and make the best use of the boss's time. The scheduler is usually responsible for making a representative or senator's travel arrangements. This includes booking and changing flights, getting proper driving directions, and arranging hotels.

A scheduler may seek an intern's assistance with coordinating directions to meetings and events or making revisions to a schedule or travel accommodations. Pay attention to how the Congress member's day is arranged, which meetings and events get on the member's schedule and why—and which don't—and which events are a priority and why.

Caseworkers

A caseworker is responsible for resolving an individual constituent's problem with the federal government or request for a federal agency's services. Typically, if the scope of the problem or request requires no change in law, regulation, or policy and is unrelated to pending federal legislation, it becomes a case, and a file is created and opened for that constituent. The caseworker is responsible for contacting the relevant federal agency or agencies and working to resolve the constituent's problem. A caseworker must have a good working knowledge of each federal agency's jurisdiction and processes, as well as contacts within many agencies who may be able to facilitate a resolution to a problem.

Caseworkers have to be well organized and persistent. They have to be compassionate and good listeners. Most cases involve people who are in desperate need of help—seniors needing help with Social Security or Medicare; veterans having problems with their Veterans Affairs (VA) benefits; families of military personnel looking for information on an injured loved one; or people having immigration and naturalization problems. Other casework may include requests to expedite a passport or visa or locate military records.

You can learn a lot from a caseworker. Offices can have as many as one hundred cases pending at any time, but typically have only one to four caseworkers to handle the work. Caseworkers must have the ability to identify which federal agency has jurisdiction over an issue, correspond with and ask for the agency's assistance, and follow up with the agency and the constituent, all in a timely manner.

Again, the work requires a tremendous knowledge of the federal agencies and their jurisdictions, good organization skills, and persistence and dogged determination to resolve problems. Casework also requires the worker to be sensitive and diplomatic with constituents and their problems. Caseworkers provide important constituent service on behalf of members of Congress, and their work is invaluable to the success of a congressional office.

The Grant Assistant/Coordinator

Another job commonly found in a district office is the grant assistant or grant coordinator. A grant assistant helps local governments, schools and universities, community groups, researchers, nonprofit organizations, and others obtain federal funding.

Grants are funds (money) given for a specific purpose directly to an individual, group, government, or organization that meets certain criteria. In most circumstances, interested parties must submit an application and compete for a grant. A grant is not a loan; it is a specific allotment of money that does not have to be repaid. The grant's purpose is usually outlined by Congress in federal law. A federal agency develops the criteria, administers the grant program, and provides the funding.

Like a caseworker, a grant assistant should have a good working knowledge of each federal agency and the programs run by each agency. He or she must know what grants are available and, more important, know the hoops, processes, and red tape one must get through when applying for a grant and competing for federal funding. It is important that a grant assistant develop reliable contacts and work closely with federal agencies to track grant applications, work through any problems with an application, and communicate to the applicant any insight on the process or progress.

This position provides a vital constituent service for the district and the elected official. Members of Congress must show that they are effective in serving their district and obtaining help for their community. If a member is successful in helping constituents get federal grants, he or she can easily demonstrate to the community his or her effectiveness as a federal legislator. When a congressional office receives notice that a constituent will be receiving a federal grant, a press release is sent to trumpet the representative or senator's success in helping win the grant.

Grant assistants utilize interns to research grants—what types are available, who can apply, what criteria are used, how much funding is available, and so forth. You should also expect to help the grant assistant work with an applicant through the application process, by contacting agencies and tracking grant applications. From a grant assistant, you can expect to learn more about how the federal government works and each agency's jurisdiction. You will utilize your writing and research skills. You can also see how, how much, and where federal tax dollars are spent.

Staff Assistants

The staff assistant position is primarily entry level. As an intern, expect to spend most of your time helping the staff assistant or assistants. They fulfill the duties of a receptionist and perform general office tasks.

The staff assistant's work may include answering telephones; opening, sorting, and time-stamping mail; making copies; assisting with thank-you notes and congratulatory and personal letters; meeting with constituents; maintaining files; and taking care of other administrative paperwork and duties. In addition, a staff assistant often processes requests for American flags that have flown over the U.S. Capitol (which can be purchased through any U.S. House or Senate office), as well as requests for special tours in Washington. They help obtain copies of legislation or other information made available by the federal government for constituents. The success of the office is largely dependent on the hard work and efficiency of the staff assistants. Considering that a staff assistant is often the first person a constituent meets at the office door or speaks with on the telephone, it is crucial that he or she interacts with constituents in a professional, courteous, and considerate manner.

Staff assistants are not expected to have in-depth knowledge of politics or the inner workings of government. Rather they need a keen understanding of their office, its functions, and their fellow workers' areas of responsibility. The staff assistant helps direct the flow of work in the office and must ensure that telephone calls, messages, and letters get to the right staff in a timely and efficient manner, with all the necessary information. Poor performance often leads to embarrassing problems and constituent complaints and is not long tolerated. In turn, good work by staff assistants enables the office staff to work efficiently and provide better service to their boss and constituents.

Again, staff assistant is usually an entry-level position that enables the employee, and the interns working with him or her, to learn the many duties and functions of a congressional office and how to properly interact with constituents. Good staff assistants are usually promoted to other staff positions when openings occur. Good work at this position is easily recognized and often rewarded with more fulfilling tasks, such as pursuing casework, assisting with scheduling, or working more closely with the district director or executive assistant.

The Interns

As an intern, you should expect to assist and fill in for the staff assistants. Your hard work and effective performance at this position will be rewarded with more interesting and fulfilling tasks. You can learn a great deal about how the office functions by observing how staff assistants do their jobs. You can learn how to listen to and talk with constituents; see what types of telephone calls, mail, and requests for information and assistance come into the office; and see how these requests are processed.

Again, most district offices throughout the country have employees performing jobs and duties similar to those listed above, often with similar titles. Although those listed cover many of the tasks performed in a district office, you can expect to find variations in job titles and scope of work.

Do's and Don'ts

Do Take an Interest in Your Work and Do Your Job Well

You will get the most out of your interning experience by simply being capable, taking an interest in your work, and acting professionally. Always keep in mind that district offices are usually understaffed, and therefore the employees want your help and hope that they can depend on you. Again, your efficient, hard work at this position will be rewarded with more interesting and fulfilling tasks.

The staff are also responsible for other tasks that can expose you to legislative and policy issues. They forward letters, comments, and inquiries on federal legislation and policy to the representative or senator's Washington, D.C., office. More important, they must be able to effectively listen to and communicate constituent views on legislation to the Washington staff.

The district staff must have a cursory knowledge of pending federal legislation and legislative priorities to discuss issues capably and communicate views to the Washington office. The staff is dependent on the Washington office to keep them apprised of developments on Capitol Hill. In addition, they utilize weekly Washington newspapers such as *The Hill* and *Roll Call* and periodicals such as the *National Journal* and *Congressional Quarterly Weekly Report* to keep abreast of events in Washington. These periodicals are available on-line as well as in hard copy.

Don't Make Ramen Noodle Soup in the Coffeepot

An intern in one of my former offices once did this—we still don't know why. It looked like a science lab experiment gone very bad. I use this example of a minor, relatively humorous offense to illustrate an important point—if you don't understand the office etiquette or policies, ask your intern coordinator or supervisor, especially before you do anything that you may regret. On any matter, when in doubt—ask.

Do Keep Your Eyes and Ears Open

Learn through observation! You will learn the most by watching and listening to what is going on around you.

Listen to how the staff talk to constituents and the media. Pay attention to the staff's discussions with constituents about legislative issues and casework. Listen to the information they share about the Congress member's schedule, local political matters, and other elected officials. If it's available, read the senator or representative's schedule. Pay attention to what local daily press articles are sent to the Washington office, and ask why. Watch how the member talks and interacts with different audiences. Read press releases and newsletters. Observe the incoming mail and telephone calls and note trends.

What Goes On in the Office Stays in the Office

What happens in the office stays in the office. Be very careful about what you tell others about what you see and hear at your internship.

Always keep in mind that you are working for a successful public figure who has worked hard to develop a public image. You have been given an opportunity to work closely—on the "inside"—with that person and will see and hear information that is not intended for public consumption. There are many people interested in using certain information to damage or ruin an elected official's career. Sharing with outsiders insight on decisions made by staff or on personal matters regarding the staff or the member of Congress, or other information that you are privy to because of your position is wrong and could be damaging—to you, the representative or senator, and the staff.

In addition, letters and telephone calls to the member of Congress and the information contained in them are personal and confidential. You should never share with others what you read in a personal letter or hear in a telephone call or meeting, nor should you share who is contacting the office. That is the business of the Congress member and his or her constituents; it is not for public knowledge.

Do Ask Questions

When you don't know what something is or how to do it—ask. When you need help—ask. If there is any confusion on any matter—ask, especially before doing something that you may regret. The staff wants your help and needs you to properly complete and perform tasks.

The district staff recognizes that your internship is an educational and learning experience. At appropriate times, ask questions that will help you understand more about office operations and processes, the Congress member's positions on issues, the legislative process, local politics, campaigns, and any of your other observations.

Do Respect the Experience of the Professional Staff

As previously stated, you will have a better internship experience by observing and, at appropriate times, asking questions. Remember that if you perform your work capably, quietly, and with interest and professionalism, you will be given duties that are more fun, interesting, and challenging.

The district staff is comprised of experienced professionals. Respect them. You can learn a lot from them. Always "mind your manners" when interacting with the legislator, the professional staff, and your fellow interns. Be a good listener and always act professionally, even if you disagree with them.

Do Be Flexible

The district staff will work with you to create your work schedule. Interns often work anywhere from ten to thirty hours a week, usually in shifts of at least three hours per day. As previously stated, district offices are understaffed, and therefore the employees want your help and hope that they can depend on you. Keep your schedule and show up to work on time.

In addition to your regular schedule, make time available and volunteer to assist with many of the office-related activities that occur outside the office. They can be fun and a welcome change to the typical "day at the office." The staff attend press conferences, constituent town meetings, ribbon cuttings, awards banquets, Rotary Club lunches, plant and business tours, and similar activities throughout the week, in the evenings, and on weekends. They attend these meetings both with and without the member of Congress.

Also, many staff members use their personal time—outside office hours—to volunteer their help at political and campaign-related events. These may include fundraisers, party meetings, debates, rallies, press conferences, and door-to-door literature drops. The district staff will welcome your willingness to help at outside-the-office events. Your participation will add to your internship by providing you new opportunities to observe the senator or representative and his or her staff interacting with the public, serving constituents, and working toward reelection. These events may also give you the chance to network with local politicians or meet prominent national figures who are in town for a special event. Furthermore, performing this "extra" work demonstrates your enthusiastic commitment to the office.

Do Remember That You Are an Intern, Not the Member of Congress

Don't confuse your values and policy preferences for those of the member of Congress. You were not elected to be an intern. You did not campaign for yourself or your position on issues. It is your boss's views, opinions, and positions on public policy and political issues that are important—not yours.

It is widely understood that, though people can usually agree on some issues, their opinions will vary on many others. You are not going to agree with every one of the Congress member's positions. What is important is not that you agree or disagree but rather that you, as a member of the staff, publicly promote, communicate, and support his or her views and opinions. This may not be easy—especially when you do not share the legislator's views on a particular matter—but it is your job.

Do Dress Professionally and Appropriately

Constituents, elected officials, and important visitors can walk into a district office at anytime. The district office staff understand that you probably lack the budget for an extensive business wardrobe, but appearance still matters. You have to be conscious of your appearance and the image that you project. Remember that you are representing the member of Congress and his or her office. Use common sense. Observe what the rest of the staff wears and try to dress accordingly. As always, when in doubt—ask.

Whatever you do, don't wear Bermuda shorts with a shirt, tie, and jacket to the office and then argue with the intern supervisor when he or she sends you home! An intern of ours who came in wearing shorts made two mistakes: First, he made the mistake of not dressing appropriately, and second, he argued with his supervisor that his choice of attire was appropriate. He was asked to not return.

Take full advantage of your internship. As a congressional intern, you have the opportunity to gain valuable insight and knowledge of our democratic, representative form of government. An internship is a nontraditional form of education; it gives you a rare chance to apply what you have learned in the classroom and to verify whether what you have been taught is true in the real world.

Enjoy interacting with the many new and different people you'll encounter: concerned citizens, politicians, major donors, local opinion leaders, members of the press, elected officials, businessmen and -women, activists, campaign supporters, the representative or senator, bureaucrats, and public servants.

Take time out to observe what is going on around you. You will learn more by watching and listening than from any work that you are asked to do.

Most of all, have fun and enjoy being away from the classroom. Your internship will expose you to new people, new ideas, and new perspectives. Make the most of it!

5

The White House Internship

Matthew Bennett
AMERICANS FOR GUN SAFETY
(FORMER DEPUTY ASSISTANT TO THE PRESIDENT
AND DEPUTY DIRECTOR OF INTERGOVERNMENTAL
AFFAIRS, THE WHITE HOUSE)

The White House: the home of presidents, the seat of power, a national icon, and the location of the most famous and notorious internship in world history. The White House is also a place where thousands before you have had exciting and rewarding internship experiences.

This chapter will take you behind the gates of the White House and give you a brief glimpse of what life is like for interns there. Though the term "White House intern" became linked for a time with presidential bad behavior, the White House internship program provides its participants with an extraordinary firsthand look at the inner sanctum of American government.

What's Inside the White House Gates

For many, the workings of the White House are deeply mysterious. This is despite the unequaled openness of the president's house—journalists report from a space a few steps away from the Oval Office; ordinary citizens can visit the White House (the *only* executive residence in the world that is open to tourists); and Hollywood has made repeated attempts to peek behind the curtain (*The American President* and *The West Wing*, for example). Still, the enormous power and momentous—and often secretive—decisionmaking that go on daily in the White House makes it a puzzling and **fascinating** place for almost all who pause to consider it.

The "18 Acres"

"The White House" means more than the mansion with the world's most famous address. The term "White House" really refers to the entire complex within the black iron gates at 1600 Pennsylvania Avenue—insiders call this the "18 Acres."

The central part of the 18 Acres is the mansion itself. This houses the first family's living quarters on the top floors, the State Floor (where formal functions like dinners take place), and the bottom floor rooms with old presidential china patterns that tourists file past for much of each day. You almost certainly will not be working in any part of the mansion. Rather, you will be in one of the working portions of the White House complex. The working spaces consist of the mansion's two attached wings and the other huge building that sits inside the White House gates, the Eisenhower Executive Office Building (EEOB). (This was called the "Old EOB" until Congress renamed it in 2000. Some old-timers still call it the OEOB.)

The West Wing

As many people know from the hit television series by the same name, the West Wing of the White House is the center of power because it contains the Oval Office. But although the TV show accurately portrays the crush of daily issues and problems facing the president and the staff, the real West Wing is almost nothing like the set you see on television. On the show, the West Wing is a nest of activity—staffers run around like manic honeybees, never seeming to communicate unless they are in motion. And the show's sprawling set makes the West Wing look like a huge law firm or newsroom.

In fact, the real West Wing is hushed, and there is little of the scurrying that the show is so fond of—most White House staffers (like office workers everywhere) communicate by phone and email. The real West Wing is also small; it has only three tiny floors, and many of the offices are cramped and windowless. In the White House—as in real estate—location matters, so many of the top White House officials choose proximity to the president and the cachet of the West Wing over the spaciousness of the offices in the EEOB.

Fans of *The West Wing* can take comfort in the fact that the show gets some things right. The Press Briefing Room set is close to realistic, and the Oval Office set looks almost exactly like the Clinton Oval. (President Bush has changed the carpet, furniture, and drapes). The Roosevelt Room (where the show's staffers have their meetings, under a large painting of Teddy Roosevelt) is fairly accurate: The portrait looks right, but the real walls are not made of glass. If you want to see what the West Wing really looks like before your internship begins, rent the movie *The American President.* Those sets are stunningly realistic.

The East Wing

The East Wing of the White House is configured differently than its more famous western cousin, but it also has working offices, including those devoted to White House visitors and tourists, as well as the Office of Legislative Affairs (the president's liaisons to Congress). The first lady also has a large staff, many of whom work out of the East Wing. (Before Hillary Clinton's time, the East Wing was known as "the First Lady's Wing." Mrs. Clinton broke tradition by having her own West Wing office.)

The EEOB

Although some interns work in the East Wing and a handful—less than a dozen—are chosen to work in the West Wing, the vast majority of White House interns work in the Eisenhower Executive Office Building (EEOB). This enormous building, with a mile and a half of corridors, is home to most of the White House staff. The building's history offers an interesting lesson on how the federal government has grown. When the building now called the EEOB was first built 130 years ago, it housed the State Department *and* the War and Navy Departments (War and Navy have since been combined in the Department of Defense). At the time, the White House staff was contained entirely within the White House mansion. Over the years, both State and Defense moved out of the EEOB to their own huge complexes, and the White House staff has continued to grow—not only filling the EEOB but sprawling outward to an array of other buildings that sit just outside the gates of the 18 Acres.

Although the White House is obviously rich in history, the EEOB is full of stories of its own: Franklin Roosevelt had an office in the EEOB as an Assistant Secretary of the Navy (it now belongs to the vice president's chief of staff), and President Nixon spent many of his days working—and yes, taping—in Room 180, which is now a conference room. You will get to know the EEOB well, because unless you are among the very few interns chosen for the East or West Wing, you will spend the days of your White House internship walking its black-and-white-checked floors.

How White House Internships Work

Working in the White House

White House staff members are professional and hardworking, and so are the interns. Dress is business attire at almost all times (there may be some casual days when the president and others are on vacation in late summer). For men, jackets must always be worn in the West Wing during business hours.

Hours for the staff are very long, but most offices do not expect interns to arrive before 8:30 A.M. or to stay past 6:00 P.M. Most interns do not work on weekends, although there may be some exceptions.

When you work in the White House, everything going on there is potentially newsworthy, and each of the day's national headlines in some way leads back to the White House. White House staff members therefore are addicted to news: Cable news blares constantly from office televisions, and everyone reads the daily "press clips," a compilation of that day's news stories from the major newspapers and other outlets that is prepared and circulated very early each morning. The staff read the major national news magazines and Capitol Hill publications like *Roll Call* and the *National Journal*. And because much of what the White House does is viewed through the lens of politics, the staff reads political publications like the *Hotline*, an Internet-based political news service.

What You Will Do (and What You Will Not Do)

It should not come as a shock to find out that, as a White House intern, you will not be called to the Situation Room for urgent national security meetings. You will not travel with the president aboard his helicopter, *Marine I*. You will not play tennis on the White House courts. What you will do is answer the phones, make copies, and write letters. You will help well-connected tourists cut the long lines at the Visitors' Entrance. You will seal envelopes, update birthday card lists, and get the soda for the office from the White House Mess. You will, in short, join your intern colleagues throughout Washington in doing a lot of administrative work.

In part, this is a structural necessity. One thing you will notice right away is that the White House is very short on secretaries (meaning the kind who type things, not the secretary of state). The president has one, and a few others do too, but most senior and mid-level staffers in the White House rely on their interns to do most of the administrative work.

Although these may appear to be small and mundane tasks, much can be learned from them. That document you copy may be the president's schedule for the day, filled with details about what he will do and see. That phone call you field might be from a state governor or corporate CEO. That letter you write might be to your own senator. Or it may be to someone's Aunt Mabel, wishing her a happy anniversary. There is no denying that some intern work is drudgery. But even if your daily tasks are somewhat dull, there is always the chance for exciting opportunities to pop up: A staffer might take you to a meeting with some famous people; you might get to help with crowd control at a state arrival ceremony on the South Lawn; or if you are very lucky, you might walk past the president in the hallway.

Moreover, if you do the mundane tasks with diligence, you may be asked to do more substantive projects. Many interns do things like research policy issues, compile voting record information on members of Congress, or even go outside the White House to help prepare presidential events. Although there are no guarantees that you will get such stimulating assignments, working hard at the small projects is certain to help bring them your way.

Office Assignment

When you are accepted into the White House internship program, you probably will be given the opportunity to list your top few preferences for the office in which you would like to work. (A brief description of the White House offices follows.) The Intern Office "aspires" to honor each applicant's requests.

Interns choose to work at the White House for a variety of reasons. Some want simply to serve a president they admire; others seek to learn about how policy is made at the top of the federal government; still others are there just for the thrill and the proximity to power. Whatever your reason for coming to the White House, do not choose your office preference based on the half-baked notion that a certain office (scheduling, advance, and the Social Office are the usual suspects) will give you the inside track to the president. This is a time-honored but totally useless exercise—many interns before you have tried to work the system to get a glimpse of The Man and have failed.

Also be prepared for disappointment. Very few interns get either their first or even second office preference. Many interns come to the White House with highly inflated expectations about where they will work and what they will do, and some quit, dissolve into tears, or perpetually lobby the Intern Office for reassignment when they are put in the Correspondence Office to run the "autopen" (the machine that signs the president's name to the vast bulk of outgoing letters.)

You should *expect* to be in the Correspondence Office—that is where the majority of interns go. Moreover, the Correspondence Office's bad reputation among incoming interns is undeserved. Let's face it, most interns in Washington handle the mail. The White House receives thousands of letters and cards every day, and they range from the ten-year-old asking about the president's dog to a prime minister raising important questions of state. These letters need to be processed and answered quickly and accurately. Although working in Correspondence may not seem like the most glamorous of postings, keep in mind that you will be putting words in the mouth of the President of the United States with your work, while interns in other offices may be making copies or answering the phone.

Access Passes

Almost everyone in the White House—staff members, interns, journalists, contractors, Secret Service agents, military personnel, visitors, and others—must wear badges with their picture, name, and status. These badges are color coded to reveal the access that person is allowed around the White House complex. For interns, the access levels range from the Orange Pass, which allows access to the EEOB, to the coveted Blue Pass, which gives (almost) full access to the entire White House complex (everywhere other than the first family's living quarters). Most White House interns are given Orange Passes. This gets you into the complex and to the areas you need to go, but it requires a Blue Pass–holder to accompany you into the White House itself.

Things to Avoid

Don't Worry About Your Pass Color

Pass colors are the subject of endless anguish and anxiety for interns. If you get an Orange Pass, as you almost certainly will, worrying about how you can get a Blue Pass is likely to waste valuable time and energy. This is a serious mistake. You will be able to see and do with your Orange Pass the same range of things available to Blue Pass interns.

Don't Whine

Try to remember that working in the White House is a privilege. If your office is not the one you wanted or your pass is the wrong color, try not to unburden yourself daily on the staff members for whom you work. This is a certain one-way ticket to even more drudgery. If you want interesting assignments and exciting opportunities, be a good sport.

Don't Break the Rules

The White House is as close as we get in this country to secular sacred ground. If you are caught breaking the rules, you will embarrass yourself and possibly the president.

Believe it or not, this is not as obvious to everyone as it may seem. One intern in the Clinton White House was lucky enough to be stationed in the West Wing. On one of the several days that the New York Yankees came to the White House as World Series champions, there was an event on the South Lawn honoring the team. This intern's luck continued, as he was invited to attend the event. But then he pressed his luck: He made his way into the White House and joined the VIP photo line with President and Mrs. Clinton. When he came up in the line, the first lady turned to him, glanced at his badge (intern badges are adorned with a large "I"), and said, in a less-than-friendly voice, "who do we have here?" That intern was never seen around the White House again.

Don't Leak

Everyone loves to be an insider, and most everyone loves to hear him- or herself talk. As a White House intern, you may have access to confidential information about policy and politics—everything from the president's speeches and schedules to his deputies' phone logs and private opinions. Do not talk about these things to anyone (particularly reporters). It is unethical, unfair, and may be illegal. It is also a one-way ticket out of the White House if you are caught.

How the White House Is Organized

The White House (and by now you know I mean the White House complex) is home to a broad array of staffers and mini-agencies. Some offices directly support the president, the vice president, or other White House "principals," dealing with their daily logistics. Others are policy offices that report to the president and the White House senior staff directly, rather than through one of the federal agencies. Collectively, the entire White House staff is called the Executive Office of the President (EOP).

Below are very short summaries of the functions of the major offices within the EOP and a description of a typical work assignment in each office. These are just examples; your work assignments could be entirely different. And all of these are in addition to the universal intern duties—answering the phones, copying, filing, running errands, and the like.

The White House website has a description of each office at http://www.whitehouse.gov/government/off-descrp.html. You will notice that the longest and most detailed description provided is that of the Correspondence Office. That is not a coincidence, since most White House interns end up there.

Oval Office Operations; Office of the Chief of Staff

These are the most sought-after jobs in the world of White House internships, and like all West Wing internships, they often are assigned to interns with some connection (political or otherwise) to high-ranking West Wing staff. Interns help keep the log of the president's activities, fill out forms when the president receives gifts from visitors, and provide administrative assistance to the chief of staff and the deputies.

Advance

Every time the president leaves the White House for an event, whether it is across the street or around the world, a team of advance staffers goes to the site to prepare the logistics and politics. Because advance teams can require up to twenty staffers for a single visit and extended trips require multiple teams, the Office of Advance must search for qualified advance people willing to take time out of their jobs to do this work. Interns help by calling prospective advance staffers and taking care of their travel needs with the help of the White House Travel Office.

Cabinet Affairs

The members of the president's cabinet are the officials at the top of the vast array of federal departments and agencies. These organizations take direction from the president in a number of ways, but the most direct is through the White House Office of Cabinet Affairs. Interns might help with keeping track of the schedules of the various cabinet members. This helps the staff ensure that all senior administration appointees are working in concert to advance the president's agenda.

Communications; Strategic Initiatives

The Communications Office is responsible for coordinating the public image of the president and the White House. It is home to the speechwriters and researchers and other staffers who work on message development. Interns might help do research or make calls to organize the daily meetings to discuss policy topics for the week. The Office of Strategic Initiatives is similar to the Communications Office, but the planning is more long term.

Counsel to the President

The counsel's office is the law firm of the White House. They do everything from the mundane, like reviewing the travel requests of staffers, to advising the president on important constitutional questions. Most of the interns in this office are law students, though a few college-age interns help out with the phones and other administrative duties.

The First Lady

Although nonelected, the first lady is one of the most important players in the White House, and she commands a fairly large staff of her own. Her office is a microcosm of the rest of the White House: She has her own chief of staff, schedulers, press office, speechwriters, and policy advisors, and staffers in other offices are expected to work on her events and activities as well as those of the president and vice president. Interns in the First Lady's Office do everything from answering her mail to helping with her scheduling.

Intergovernmental Affairs

The Office of Intergovernmental Affairs acts as the president's liaison to all state and local elected officials (governors, mayors, county executives, and others). Interns in this office might make phone calls to local elected officials in a town that the president is planning to visit, inviting them to greet the president upon arrival and giving them the relevant details on the trip's logistics.

Legislative Affairs

The Office of Legislative Affairs is responsible for communications between the White House and members of Congress and their staffs. Interns in this office handle requests from the Senate and House offices for things like White House tour tickets, and they may also do research on member voting records.

Administration

The Office of Administration (OA) is responsible for the actual operations of the White House, from staff salaries and benefits to office supplies. OA also supervises several departments that serve the operational needs of the White House staff, such as the Travel Office, the Photo Office, the Visitors Office, and most important, the White House Internship Program. *(So be nice to the OA staff!)* Interns in OA help with these administrative operations, like booking travel for White House staff members and ordering photos for the people who have had their picture taken with the president.

National Security Council; Office of Homeland Security

The National Security Council (NSC) is the foreign policy and defense side of the White House. The national security advisor is, along with the secretaries of state and defense, the principal foreign policy and defense advisor to the president. Given this huge area of responsibility, it is not surprising that the NSC staff is almost as large and diversified (by issue area, region, etc.) as the rest of the White House staff combined. Because they handle classified information, everyone working for the NSC must undergo an extensive background check, a process that takes many months.

NSC internships are therefore usually limited to graduate students. The application process is lengthy and difficult, so plan far in advance.

NSC slots are highly sought after. If you are interested in NSC (or the relatively new Office of Homeland Security), try to find a connection to someone on the inside. You might start with professors you know, particularly those involved in international affairs. The senior people in NSC often move back and forth between academia and government, depending on which party is in power, so the faculty at your school may have connections. If you strike out on campus, you might try friends (or friends of friends) in congressional offices: They might know someone that could arrange an NSC interview.

Domestic Policy Office; National Economic Council

The Office of Domestic Policy handles issues like education, crime, health care, and welfare, and its sister organization, the National Economic Council, covers areas like tax policy and trade. Both are responsible for working in coordination with the relevant agencies on developing policy ideas and implementing the president's strategy in their areas of expertise. Interns in those offices may do library or Internet research on policy projects.

Political Affairs

The Office of Political Affairs is a strange beast. Created by President Reagan, Political Affairs is housed within the EOP and staffed with government employees using government resources, with the sole mission of serving the political interests of the president and his political allies and party. Although to some extent almost *all* White House employees are political hires doing work that involves partisan politics, no other government office is so blatantly, exclusively partisan. Interns in this office do research on political candidates and developments for inclusion in the weekly political briefing for the president and the senior staff. Interns should avoid this office if they do not share the president's political views.

Presidential Personnel

The Office of Presidential Personnel has a confusing name in that it has *nothing* to do with staffing the White House itself. Rather, this office sends lists of potential hires to the federal agencies to fill the political job slots in their offices. Presidential Personnel also helps fill the jobs on the many federal boards and commissions that report to the president. Interns in this office help keep track of the thousands of résumés and other information from job seekers and help coordinate hiring all over the federal government.

Press Office

The Press Office is considered one of the most glamorous intern assignments in the White House, if only because the office is the most visible. The office serves both the press secretary, who is the president's public face and voice, as well as the dozens of reporters, producers, camera crews, and others who make up the permanent White House press corps. The press corps actually works in the West Wing, in a small warren of cubbyholes behind and below the Briefing Room. It is the job of the Press Office staff and interns to keep the press informed about the day's events. Interns make and distribute copies of schedules and speeches and occasionally help shepherd the press to events within the complex.

Public Liaison

The Office of Public Liaison does outreach to organized groups, like labor, religious, ethnic, or other constituency organizations. Its staff set up White House meetings and briefings, process scheduling requests (such as letters asking the president to speak at a conference), and handle important correspondence to or from the leaders of these organizations. Interns can expect an experience similar to the other liaison offices—help with scheduling and event management (that is, keeping the lists).

Scheduling

The Scheduling Office is responsible for the most valuable commodity in the White House: the president's time. The director of scheduling works out the basic blocks of time in a given month, and detailed daily schedules are produced by one of the four deputy schedulers. This office has constant contact with almost every other part of the White House because all offices want the president to spend time on their issues, their constituents, or their staff. Interns in Scheduling help respond to the large volume of mail that comes in asking for presidential visits, and they keep updated versions of the schedules flowing to every corner of the White House.

Social Office

The Social Office is responsible for all events that occur within the White House or on the grounds. Social Office staffers work for weeks on major events, like state dinners (where the first family hosts visiting heads of state), and handle traditional events, like the White House holiday parties and the Easter Egg Roll. Interns do a lot of list-keeping work for the bigger events, making invitation calls and manning phones on the RSVP lines.

Staff Secretary/Correspondence

The staff secretary is responsible for perhaps the *second* most valuable commodity in the White House: the flow of paper to the president. This office prepares the president's daily briefing book and coordinates other paper flow, like bill signings and official proclamations. The staff secretary also oversees the part of the operation to which White House interns are most likely to be assigned—the Correspondence Office. Correspondence interns help open, sort, read, and respond to the huge volume of letters, cards, emails, and faxes that come in daily to the president.

Office of the Vice President

Like the First Lady's, the Vice President's office (OVP) is a microcosm of the entire White House: OVP has its own chief of staff, scheduling, advance, counsel, correspondence, and so forth. The OVP staff is spread out: The vice president has offices in the West Wing, the EEOB (where most of the staff works), and the Naval Observatory (the vice president's home). Plus, in his capacity as president of the Senate, the vice president has offices and staff in the Capitol Building (*two* offices just off the Senate floor and another on the House side) and in a Senate office building. Interns work in all areas of the OVP, and their experiences vary, but many have commented that the smaller offices in OVP sometimes afford them more substantive work opportunities than their friends have gotten in other parts of the White House. Nevertheless, most of the time they answer phones and sort the mail.

Alphabet Soup: The Other White House Policy Shops

In addition to the offices listed above, the EOP is home to a variety of offices that deal with more specific policy areas. Because this is government, these tend to go by their acronyms, which are largely self-explanatory: CEA (Council of Economic Advisors); CEQ (Council on Environmental Quality); ONDCP (Office of National Drug Control Policy—the "drug czar"); OSTP (Office of Science and Technology Policy), and others. Plus there is the massive OMB (Office of Management and Budget), the huge agency within the White House responsible for supervising the budgets and regulatory work of the various federal departments. Most of these offices use interns for largely the same tasks as the other policy offices.

Final Notes

If you are lucky enough to land a White House internship, be sure to take the time to take it all in. Remember that you might never again have the good fortune to stride through those big black gates. Regardless of the task you are assigned, your sheer proximity to power guarantees a rewarding experience if you do it right: Play by the rules, do what's asked of you, and keep your eyes open, and you are almost certain to have an experience you will remember forever.

6

The Executive Branch Internship

Brett Heindl
SYRACUSE UNIVERSITY

The federal executive branch is sprawling and complicated. It occupies hundreds of buildings, processes information from thousands of offices, employs tens of thousands of people, and commands a budget of literally trillions of dollars. The executive branch's sheer enormity makes it impossible to cover the whole range of experiences in a single chapter. Rather than giving you a list of rules to follow and steps to take, this chapter will instead show you what questions to ask so that you can figure out the answers on your own. So if this chapter repeats one lesson over and over again, it is to keep your eyes open and pay attention to the things going on around you. This may not seem earth-shaking advice. However, this chapter will make those first weeks a little easier by giving you a better idea of what things to pay attention to and by taking some of the mystery out of the early part of the experience.

If you're reading this chapter, you probably have a fairly positive view of federal executive-branch bureaucracy. Indeed, some of the most passionate, intelligent, and genuinely nice people work in the executive branch. Internships in the executive agencies can be among the most rewarding experiences available to students hoping to get a foot in the door of the policy-making world. Not only do you have a chance to do work that is intellectually stimulating, dealing with and trying to solve real-world problems in real time, but you also make decisions that will affect hundreds if not thousands of people in the nation and the world. The sense of responsibility that accompanies this power will undoubtedly change the way you look at the government and the real people who implement the policies, administer the programs, and run the offices within the executive branch.

The Executive Branch

The executive branch's complexity is due partly to the wide array of issues that the bureaucracy addresses and partly to the ad hoc way it has evolved over the last 220 years. A member of the cabinet heads each agency and presents its perspective in meetings with the president. The president delegates to the administrative agencies the power to execute laws enacted by Congress. Because these laws are often vague and mutually contradictory, the executive agencies have considerable latitude in interpreting and implementing them. This is a source of conflict and suspicion between the legislative and executive branches.

Congress exercises a great deal of power over the executive agencies by virtue of its oversight function and its control over the budget. Agency officials frequently testify before congressional committees about their activities and about particular policy situations. The oversight and budgetary functions are very important in maintaining accountability for the nonelected officials who make up the agencies. However, Congressional involvement can make life within the agencies very stressful by further politicizing the policy-making process. Although they grumble about it, the people within the executive branch take their interactions with Congress very seriously, because, within the agencies, positive relations with Capitol Hill are a matter of survival.

The executive agencies often squabble among themselves too. Some tensions between the agencies are the result of turf wars (which agency has the lead on issue X), personal rivalries, or differences in organizational culture. For example, some people in the Department of Defense (DOD) think that the Department of State is full of hand-wringing, Chardonnay-sipping intellectuals, whereas some in the State Department think that the DOD is full of mouth breathers and knuckle draggers. On some level, this competition is understandable, because people working for different agencies often come from different backgrounds that emphasize certain traits over others. In the above example, the conflict between State and the DOD results from different organizational cultures and different, but overlapping, missions. Because of its focus on military matters, the DOD emphasizes hierarchy and efficiency and approaches foreign policy questions from a military perspective. The State Department, by contrast, because it deals in diplomacy and negotiation, is more open to speculation and consensus seeking. Diplomats abhor direct confrontation, whereas soldiers accept it (as long as it's well planned).

This tension is inevitable, but it isn't necessarily a bad thing. If well managed, it generates a creativity and stimulates critical thinking. This is clear if you compare the bureaucracy to the American legal system. Decision making in the bureaucracy resembles a courtroom in that it is based on the principle that the best option will emerge through an adversarial process. In an adversarial process, each side must present better evidence and more plausible arguments, while overcoming the other side's continual attacks on its weaknesses, to achieve its policy preference. This process also helps to maintain some unity within the administration by building consensus. It lessens the acrimony between agencies that could affect future interagency cooperation or could prevent coherent policy implementation.

Typically, executive branch agencies are organized hierarchically, although the realities are always a bit more complex. The Department of Defense is notoriously centralized, while the Departments of Justice and Energy are notoriously decentralized, with the head not always aware of what the limbs are doing. The other agencies usually fall somewhere in between, with the branch offices subordinate to the Washington, D.C., headquarters. Each agency has its own peculiar organizational chart, so rather than my explaining the exact makeup and function of each agency and subdivision (referred to hereafter as a "bureau"), you would be better served by looking at each agency's website. However, the agencies' basic structures are similar enough if you look at the bureaucracy as an enormous filter.

The head of each agency represents the administration on certain policy issues. For example, the secretary of state represents the president on all matters relating to foreign policy, while the secretary of health and human services deals with matters relating to the well-being of all Americans. In order to perform this function, these agency heads must have a sophisticated understanding of an enormous range of issues. However, every person has his or her limits, so there must be some filtration process whereby the agency head deals only with the most pressing concerns and delegates authority over the less important issues to other people. Therefore, each agency operates as a highly specialized entity that processes a great deal of information while filtering the amount going to the top. So the farther down the organizational pyramid you look, the more highly specialized is the information processed and generated by the office or individual. Most people at the lower levels have a large volume of knowledge about a narrow range of issues with which they deal exclusively. In addition to the people working on policy issues, a roughly equivalent number of people carry out the administrative tasks necessary for the agency's continued functioning. The administrators do the hiring and firing, generate the payroll, order office supplies, and schedule meetings and coordinate itineraries. They supply the grease that keeps the bureaucracy moving. Figures 6.1 and 6.2 show the organizational structures of the Departments of Health and Human Services and Defense.

Where Do Interns Fit In?

Federal agencies recognize the importance of interns and consequently devote considerable attention to developing their internship programs. In the end, both interns and administrators benefit from the internship experience. Interns acquire valuable experience and a taste for a specific line of work, while the agencies use the cheap labor to carry some of the workload. An agency also uses

Figure 6.1 U.S. Department of Health and Human Services

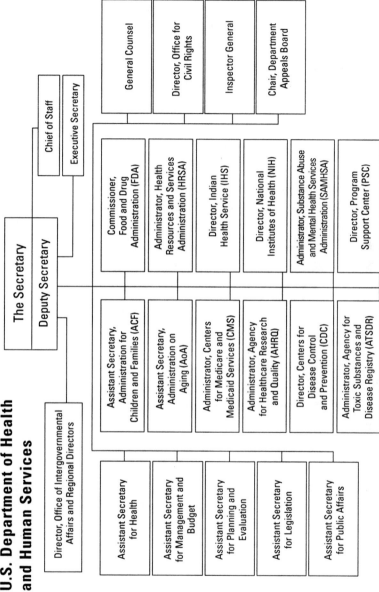

internships to recruit fresh talent and to interest smart, ambitious people in careers in the agency. In terms of intern placement, in most cases, executive branch agencies accept applications for specific bureaus within the agency. From there, bureau administrators determine the number of interns that they can accommodate. This number is usually based on the facilities they have available and the amount of extra help they need. Budgetary concerns do factor into this allocation process, since although most interns are unpaid, they still cost the bureau money and resources. Interns must be trained and given access to a computer and a desk. On top of that, the bureau has to pay people to process the paperwork and manage the additional logistics of taking on an extra five to seven people for the summer. Interns' duties may range from menial tasks like filing and photocopying to more substantive work like drafting policy recommendations and writing reports.

Real Work, Not Busy Work

Most undergraduate internships involve a good bit of relatively mundane tasks, although each placement contains the possibility of more substantive work. In my case, as a graduate student, I was fortunate enough to be placed in an office that was noticeably short staffed. Because of my previous experience and level of education, I was assigned to a specific policy portfolio and for three months was designated "the go-to guy" for all matters related to that portfolio. However, others' experiences—at both the graduate and undergraduate levels—were more uneven.

My observations yielded two main points. First, there is a degree of luck involved. Naturally, some intern positions are more exciting than others. This uncertainty can be frustrating because it sometimes takes a few weeks to see whether you have a good one or a dud. Second, even if you're stuck in an internship that doesn't seem very interesting, ambition and hard work can be the difference between pushing paper and doing something more interesting. If you demonstrate your enthusiasm and attention to detail for the smaller projects and administrative tasks, you will earn the trust of your

Figure 6.2 Office of the Secretary of Defense

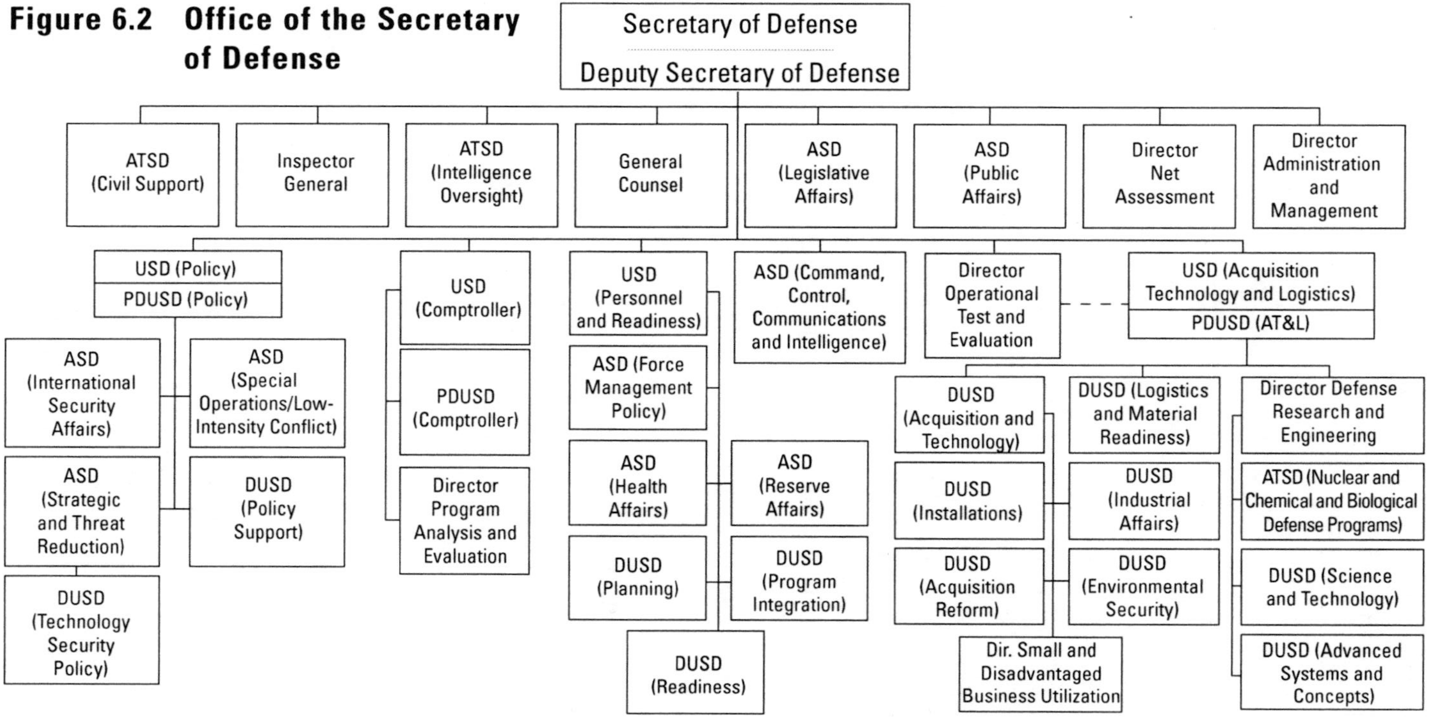

Secretary of Defense

Deputy Secretary of Defense

- ATSD (Civil Support)
- Inspector General
- ATSD (Intelligence Oversight)
- General Counsel
- ASD (Legislative Affairs)
- ASD (Public Affairs)
- Director Net Assessment
- Director Administration and Management

USD (Policy)
PDUSD (Policy)
- ASD (International Security Affairs)
- ASD (Special Operations/Low-Intensity Conflict)
- ASD (Strategic and Threat Reduction)
- DUSD (Policy Support)
- DUSD (Technology Security Policy)

USD (Comptroller)
- PDUSD (Comptroller)
- Director Program Analysis and Evaluation

USD (Personnel and Readiness)
- ASD (Force Management Policy)
- ASD (Health Affairs)
- DUSD (Planning)
- ASD (Reserve Affairs)
- DUSD (Program Integration)
- DUSD (Readiness)

ASD (Command, Control, Communications and Intelligence)

Director Operational Test and Evaluation

USD (Acquisition Technology and Logistics)
PDUSD (AT&L)
- DUSD (Acquisition and Technology)
- DUSD (Logistics and Material Readiness)
- DUSD (Installations)
- DUSD (Industrial Affairs)
- DUSD (Acquisition Reform)
- DUSD (Environmental Security)
- Dir. Small and Disadvantaged Business Utilization
- Director Defense Research and Engineering
- ATSD (Nuclear and Chemical and Biological Defense Programs)
- DUSD (Science and Technology)
- DUSD (Advanced Systems and Concepts)

colleagues and put yourself in a stronger position to ask for more substantive work.

Communicate Your Expectations

The best way to ensure a positive experience is to sit down with your supervisor on the first day and make sure both of you understand your position within the office. This way, you can get an idea of what his or her expectations for you are, and you can play a part in shaping those expectations while they are still flexible. In addition, there will be fewer chances for misunderstanding in the coming months. When receiving your job description, get as many details as possible: What hours will you work? When will your internship end? What projects will you be working on? What are the deadlines and timetables for those projects? How often should you meet with the supervisor to evaluate your progress, and for how long? Be honest and frank about your expectations: Do you want to do policy work, or are you more comfortable with administrative work? Would you rather work on a large number of small projects or a few big ones? Are the supervisor's expectations for you realistic? Do they make the most of your talents? Express your interests and career goals and discuss how you would like to work them into the internship experience. Be ambitious; this is your chance to get your foot in the door for meaningful projects. If well conducted, these initial meetings with your supervisor will set the tone for the rest of your internship. Again, the best thing to do is to establish a clear, frank line of communication with your supervisor and your coworkers in the early days.

If everyone understands that you have specific projects to work on, everyone will know that you are not content to be the photocopy lackey. When I was working summer jobs in college, I learned one crucial lesson that applies to any job: If you don't want to get stuck with grunt work, look busy. If you don't have a few projects going on at once, the people around you will think that you're available to do the boring, brainless jobs that they don't want to do, like photocopying, data entry, and filing. Granted, as the low person on the totem pole, you probably can't avoid all of that kind of work, but you can certainly minimize the time spent doing it if you show hard work and initiative.

Dress for Success

At many executive branch agencies, people dress fairly formally. Some agencies are different (the U.S. Agency for International Development [USAID] and the Departments of Labor and Agriculture come to mind), but in most, the standard dress for both men and women is a suit, and haircuts are conservative. Interns often stand out because their hair is too long, they have too much facial hair, or they are underdressed. Although this is true for most interns, it is especially true for men. Most college-age men are not used to paying attention to those things and think that suits are meant only for weddings or funerals. Also most interns do not have the money to buy extra clothes that will sit in a closet for the rest of the year. Finally, many just don't know the standards for dress in a federal agency and therefore fall back on what they already have.

The best way to avoid looking like an intern is to identify the things that make you look like a college student. Age is usually a dead giveaway, but since there isn't much you can do to hide that, the next best thing is to look at the other visual cues that give you away: your haircut, the way you dress, and the way you talk. Since the unofficial dress code varies according to agency and office, there is no right answer for how to dress for your internship. The best thing to do for your first week or two is to err on the side of conservatism, even if it means a different hairstyle. After a week or so, you should have a good sense of how your coworkers and, more important, your boss, dress. Remember, in this case, being treated as an equal (or near equal) by your boss and coworkers is more important than impressing your fellow interns.

Be a Professional

One of the hardest things about the transition from school to work is figuring out what it means to be a professional. Once again there is no single answer to this question. It's like good art: most people know it when they see it but can't put their finger on what separates it from the rest. Naturally, being a professional means different things to different people, but most would probably agree that the most important qualities are honesty, integrity, and hard work. However, it is difficult to translate these guidelines into daily life. The best way to flesh out these principles is to pay attention to the people around you. Identify someone in your office who seems to be a leader. Then, watch him or her closely and try to identify why that person is a strong presence in the office and why people respect him or her. Then, try to incorporate these qualities into the way you conduct yourself around the office. In time, you'll probably see that person doing things that you disagree with. No one should slavishly imitate others; ultimately, you should try to pick up the best elements of the people around you and integrate them into your own personality to develop your own distinctive brand of professionalism.

One woman in an office I interned in, Helen,[1] impressed me early on as intelligent, articulate, and opinionated, with an impressive ability to identify other actors' interests in a particular policy issue. She expressed her opinions forcefully in staff meetings and was a strong presence in the office. However, too often this forcefulness made her combative and condescending to her coworkers and subordinates. Another person in the office, Bill, was more soft-spoken but no less ambitious or informed. Rather than pushing his points, he relied on insightful comments and a broader perspective to get his points across. Finally, our office director, John, who had a very strong command of the issues as well as the political ramifications of different alternatives, often sat back and listened to the competing voices, offering counterarguments and his own opinions when appropriate. By watching the three of them, I learned a great deal about how to argue persuasively for a particular point while keeping an eye on the bigger picture. I privately critiqued the way each person did things and considered what I would do differently if I were in his or her position. I tried to draw elements from each person's office demeanor that I thought were compatible with my personality to develop my own leadership style and sense of professional ethics.

Professionalism Within the Agency

There are other important things to know about how to do your job. First, even though everyone is ostensibly under the same roof, bureaus within each agency often clash on policy issues. Again, although this will give you headaches, it is not necessarily dysfunctional, since the adversarial process theoretically ensures that the best policy option emerges. To ensure that key players within the agency have an opportunity to weigh in on an issue, all policy proposals must be forwarded to all relevant offices, then revised according to their comments. In addition to promoting the adversarial process, this procedure also keeps the other offices informed about what is going on regarding a particular issue. That way, there won't be any surprises on the horizon, and the relevant offices cannot dodge responsibility for the policy. During a typical day, an experienced policymaker may "clear" several different documents. Most clearances are merely a matter of routine, but occasionally serious conflicts erupt, demanding either extensive revision or a retraction and taking up considerable time. So when working on a specific project, make sure you pass your ideas on to other people to keep them in the loop and get their input.

Dealing with Your Boss

The review and revision cycle described above means that the people in charge wade through a great deal of paperwork every day. Therefore, if you have something that you think your supervisor or office director should review, before sending the document, go over it several times to fix its obvious weaknesses. That way, your boss can approve it after one or two revisions, rather than ten, saving him or her time for other work. On a related note, because bosses usually have more important things to do than read your fifth draft, it isn't always appropriate to give them deadlines. In yet another rookie mistake, I forwarded the final copy of a thoroughly reviewed and revised document to the assistant secretary, the head of our bureau, for a final approval. I attached a note requesting that he review and clear the document by the end of the following day so I could pass it on to the Department of Justice. Early the next day, I received an email clearing the document. Attached to it was a small note from his deputy politely informing me that giving him a deadline "wasn't kosher" and that I should refrain from doing so in the future. Another lesson learned. During the first few weeks, before sending anything to your higher-ups, be sure to have a coworker read over it to make sure your tone and language are appropriate.

The Outside World

Because I was in charge of one portfolio for the duration of my internship, I was involved in a number of intense debates about a particular policy. Two bureaus within the State Department repeatedly opposed it on the grounds that it would undermine our relations with the region. Our bureau, however, argued in favor of it, saying that it would have a negligible effect on our partnerships and that we had a humanitarian duty to invoke the policy. Finally, in July, we convened a meeting within the State Department to settle on an official position that we could present at a later meeting with the Immigration and Naturalization Service (INS) and the advocate community. We had spent two weeks preparing for the first meeting, hoping to put together an airtight case in favor of the policy. When the day arrived, debate in the conference room was intense, with our office director, John, arguing passionately in favor of the policy. After forty-five minutes of discussion, the people in charge decided that there was no compromise solution possible and that, until the issue could be brought to their higher-ups, the official State Department position would be that the matter was under review. Frustrated, we left the room and started preparing for the meeting at the INS the following week. When that day arrived, we presented our position to the advocate community, which was incensed that the State Department had not yet approved the policy. As they hurled questions at us, John, who a week before had argued so strongly in favor of the policy, now fired back with the same counterarguments that he had faced. In the end, his final message to the advocate community was this: The State Department could not approve the policy until someone found a way to answer the counterarguments. In the cab back to the State Department, John said, "For as strongly as I feel about that policy, my opinions don't matter. Until State reaches a unified decision about it, we have to keep our opinions to ourselves."

The tricky thing about dealing with the outside world—whether you're dealing with politicians, ordinary citizens, members of nonprofit organizations, or other bureaucrats—is that you are no longer just speaking as an individual; you're also speaking as a part of the administration. That means your personal opinions have to take a back seat. Unfortunately, this comes up often. When discussing policy matters outside your agency, you cannot express your own opinion freely. This is especially true if you disagree with the administration's position or if you are only partially informed about its position. There are some ways around this—you obviously won't agree with the administration on everything. But these ways are probably riskier than the alternative, which involves learning the language of politics—bland platitudes. You might be able to get away with saying that there is some debate within the administration about a particular policy, that some believe one thing and others believe another, so long as you are very careful to present both sides equally. But the only time this is permissible is in cases where the administration has not made a final decision on the issue. If a decision has been made, expressing an opposing opinion would probably get you into trouble. Sometimes you have to fall back on bland statements, such as "We're examining the situation very closely" or "We need to gather more information before we can make a decision."

You have to remember that you are representing your agency and the administration as a whole. The people you talk to about policy issues all have their own political agendas, so if you deviate from the administration's official position, you risk giving that person ammunition to use in later debates. That's what makes Washington challenging: You have to keep up your guard when talking to strangers about policy, because you don't always know that person's interest. This is why it's risky to express your own opinion too freely. To the person on the other end of the phone or across the table, you *are* the administration, and if you say that you support or oppose a particular policy, they may take that as the official position. Avoid inadvertently issuing a policy statement. Even if your listener doesn't take it that far, you don't want that person to turn to someone else in your agency the next day and say, "Well, Brett Heindl told me that his bureau thinks that . . . "

When it comes to Capitol Hill, most bureaus have one or two people designated for dealing with Congress. They know whom to talk to, whom to avoid, what to say, and how to say it. If you have to do anything involving the Hill, only do so under the supervision of your bureau's Congressional liaison. As they say in police dramas, anything you say can and will be used against you—and your bureau. I once made the mistake of asking a member of an advocacy group for a certain statistic. When he asked why I needed it, I replied that it might be an important thing to know in making a policy determination. I thought at the time that that had been a pretty innocuous answer to a loaded question. However, in a meeting several weeks later, he charged the administration with having its priorities wrong, citing my request for that statistic. When it comes to talking to people outside your agency, be careful.

Security Clearances

Many internships in national security agencies require a security clearance and a background check. Agencies that fall in this category include the Departments of State and Defense, the National Security Council (NSC), the intelligence agencies, and the Federal Bureau of Investigation, although positions in other agencies may also require them. Chances are, as an intern, you won't need a high-level clearance, so you won't have to jump through as many hoops. However, the Central Intelligence Agency and Defense Intelligence Agency both require Top Secret clearances and therefore require a very thorough background check, including personal interviews and polygraph tests. A standard clearance application focuses on three main points: your loyalty to the U.S. government, your propensity for risk-taking behavior, and your susceptibility to blackmail. Most of the questions revolve around whether you've ever associated with or participated in groups that have conspired to overthrow the U.S. government, whether you've ever used illegal drugs, and whether you've ever had significant financial problems. Again, they're concerned about whether you'll take actions that would harm national security, such as passing classified information to other countries for money, to avoid public embarrassment, or due to mental illness or chemical dependence.

The security clearance process probably raises one big question: what to do if you've ever used illegal substances. Although this seems like a difficult issue, it isn't. Do not, under any circumstances, lie on a security clearance form. It might be tempting to try to conceal past transgressions, but there are four things to keep in mind. First, your past use of illegal drugs will not automatically disqualify you for a security clearance. It will make the clearance process more complicated, but you will have a chance to explain your actions and to plead your case. I knew several people with past transgressions who still received a security clearance. Second, even if you are denied a security clearance, most agencies will be able to find a position for you that requires no access to classified material. These positions, often administrative, might not be your first choice, but they can still be rewarding experiences. Third, knowingly falsifying or concealing a material fact on a national security clearance application is a felony, punishable by fines of up to $10,000 or five years' imprisonment, or both. At the very least, if your lie is found out, your clearance will be revoked immediately. It significantly reduces the possibility that you will ever get another clearance or get another job in the federal government. Fourth, these procedures are in place for a reason. A background check is intended to determine your integrity and vulnerability to coercion or manipulation. If you have skeletons in your closet, it is best to disclose them to determine whether they could jeopardize national security.

If you are working in one of the national security agencies, do not share classified information with your friends, no matter how much you trust them. The agencies take security very seriously. In fact, your security officer will probably inform you that when handling classified information, you forfeit your right to privacy and that you should behave as if someone were constantly looking over your shoulder. Disclosing classified information to an unauthorized person, even accidentally, is a felony and carries with it very stiff penalties. Besides, most classified information is not as interesting as you might think. A large portion of information is designated classified to conceal the way it was gathered rather than its specific content. For example, Saddam Hussein's grocery list would probably be very highly classified, not so much because the information it contains is so shocking but because of the importance of protecting the identity of the person who obtained the list. Take no chances with classified information. In the end, paranoia can be your friend.

Final Thoughts

Internships in the executive branch can be both highly rewarding and highly stressful. However, if you ask the right questions, pay attention to the right people, and couple common sense with ambition, you will have a very successful internship. To boil it all down, the following guidelines will point you in the right direction:

- Work hard on all tasks and push your supervisor to give you real projects.
- Establish a frank and open line of communication with your supervisor in the early days of your internship.
- Make sure you know what your supervisor expects from you. Make sure he or she understands what you expect from him or her.
- Look busy to avoid grunt work.
- To be treated like a professional, look like a professional.
- If you think you're being underutilized, ask for a transfer.

- Identify leadership qualities and work them into your office persona.
- When writing reports or recommendations, include all relevant parties in the review process. Don't leave anyone out.
- Don't bombard your supervisor or other higher-ups with unnecessary questions. They have enough to do.
- Don't give your superiors deadlines.
- When speaking to people outside the administration, be careful: Anything you say can and will be used against you.
- Never lie on a security clearance form and never divulge classified information to unauthorized persons. Ever.

For Further Reading

For interesting illustrations of the inner workings of executive branch agencies, you might want to look at the following books: Anthony Lake, *Somoza Falling*—an insider's perspective on the decision-making process leading up to U.S. involvement in the *Sandinista* rebellion in Nicaragua. It provides a nuanced reading of the deliberations and the personalities behind them, as well as an accurate depiction of everyday life in the State Department and the NSC.

H. R. McMaster, *Dereliction of Duty*—a very thorough and compelling discussion of the Johnson administration's decisions to escalate the Vietnam War. Although highly critical of the Pentagon and the Joint Chiefs of Staff, it portrays a very turbulent period in the defense bureaucracy.

W. Henry Lambright, *Powering Apollo*—a biography of an extremely talented civil servant, James Webb, the book roots his story in the larger tale of the evolution of the National Aeronautics and Space Administration and the executive agencies in the post–World War II era.

Notes

1. This and the following names are pseudonyms.

7

The State Legislative Internship

The Honorable Joan K. Christensen
NEW YORK STATE ASSEMBLY

and *Sandra L. Davis*
EXECUTIVE ASSISTANT TO JOAN K. CHRISTENSEN

Our New York State legislative office has seen many interns over the years. As we reflected on our experiences and gathered for this chapter the lessons that we've learned over the years, we were intimately reconnected with how civically enriching the internship experience can be, both for us as supervisors and for the student interns. We finished this chapter even more confident that every college student should have some kind of political internship before graduation. There is probably no better form of civic education than what is found in actually doing politics.

One of the particular advantages of the state-level internship is that, because the offices are relatively less thoroughly staffed in comparison with Congress, there is often more work "of substance" more readily available to the intern. Indeed, many of our students with experience at both the national and state levels have made similar observations.

The material we present in this chapter is grounded in our own particular experiences in New York State; however, the advice you find here is broadly applicable to state legislative internships across the nation.

How to Select a State Legislator: It Can Be Your Choice!

Most state legislators eagerly welcome student interns because they offer fresh ideas, enthusiasm, and "free" labor. Although you may already have secured your internship, from a state perspective, there are some selection tricks and tips that might help you in the long run to feel both philosophically and politically compatible with your assignment.

Although you do not necessarily have to choose legislators by their political party, you would be wise to select a representative whose political views reasonably match yours. Because you may on occasion be asked to relay the legislator's position on a piece of legislation or a vote that was taken, feeling comfortable philosophically is always helpful. You may wish to check out a prospective legislator ahead of time by asking for a biography or a few flyers mailed out to constituents. You should watch for press releases, letters to the editor, and mailers from his or her office. If you have access to a computer, you can check out the legislator's website and voting record. Do your research ahead of time to avoid any potential embarrassment later on. This will also help prepare you for your initial contact and a subsequent interview in the legislator's office.

The Initial Contact

After you have made your selection, you should draft a brief cover letter to accompany your prepared résumé. The cover letter should clearly state who you are, why you are seeking an internship, for when and how long, and how best to contact you. Your résumé should highlight your education, interests and extracurricular activities, and future goals. It is always wise to follow up the letter and résumé with a personal phone call, just in case the letter got lost in the stack of mail that often piles up. Do not feel bad if you do not get through directly to the legislator. There are usually key staff members assigned to do the initial screening and oversight of prospective interns.

The Interview

It is vitally important that you do your homework ahead of time. At the very least you should know the responsibilities of the office: What does a state legislator do? Specifically, you should have a general idea of what this particular legislator does, his or her interests, and the nature of the district.

If you are called for an interview—most legislators require one—make sure that you are on time and dressed appropriately. Dress professionally. Jeans, shorts, T-shirts, and tank tops are *not* considered appropriate dress. You should prepare a list of thoughtful questions to ask during the process. You should have thought through not only what you intend to get out of the internship but also what you are capable of contributing. You should be able to provide legislators or their representatives highlights of your skills, strengths, and interests. You should be prepared to communicate clearly and to look interested and enthusiastic. Do not expect the interviewer to do all the talking. Know when you will be able to start the internship and what hours you are prepared to work. You need to establish a work routine that meshes into the office's general schedule. It is better, both for the legislative office staff and you, to work longer blocks of time two or three times per week than to do brief hourly stints here and there.

Before leaving the interview session, if you have not already been told that you have been selected for the position, clarify with the legislator or staff member when you may expect to receive an answer and who will contact whom. It never hurts to follow up the interview with a thank-you note the next day.

The Three Faces of a State Internship

There are three basic types of state legislative internship: the capitol experience, the district office experience, and the campaign experience. Each of these venues offers unique opportunities and challenges. Of course, it may be that you will participate in all three, particularly if it's an election year.

The Capitol Experience

You may work directly at the capitol, where the legislature meets and where bills are drafted, debated, and voted on. Most of the time you will be in the background, manning the office, greeting visitors, assisting with constituent complaints or concerns, and performing administrative tasks. You may also assist the legislator in tracking his or her legislative agenda (bill tracking).

Although each state has its own process for proposing and crafting legislation, most states follow the same basic procedure. In New York, for example, legislators introduce a series of bills (prospective laws) during the legislative session. These may be proposals addressing constituents' concerns or bills suggested by lobbying organizations. Legislators submit their ideas to their respective bill drafters (individuals who put ideas into formal legal language). Once the bill is appropriately worded, the legislator, also called the prime sponsor, circulates the draft legislation, seeking support and additional sponsors. Following circulation, the bill is then submitted to the appropriate oversight committee for review, prior to any action by the whole legislative body.

An intern might keep track of all the legislator's bills. Most legislative offices have a system to chart and follow the legislator's legislative agenda, via file cards or a bill spreadsheet or on a computer file. As an intern, you would keep a record of the assigned bill number; the list of cosponsors; the bill memorandum, highlighting the legislation's main points and justification; a copy of the full draft of the bill, with any amendments; and the bill fact sheet, containing the purposes of the provisions, which lobby groups or individuals support and which oppose the bill, and which committee is presently reviewing the bill.

Other capitol duties you may expect to perform include policy research, committee work, budget review, session debate preparation, session calendar review, and bulk constituent mailings and form letters. Occasionally there are significant policy issues requiring extensive research in preparation for either legislative debate or a critical vote in committee or on the floor of the legislature. Your legislator may ask you to do the research through the Internet, at the legislative library, through the legislative retrieval research network, or by contacting a bill's sponsor or pertinent lobby group. Your research may cover a wide range of issues from current adoption law to animal rights, from snowmobile to zebra mussel regulations. Your work and the information you collect may pay off in the passing of a significant piece of legislation affecting state residents for years to come.

Policy research may also be required to prepare the legislator to defend the bill in a floor debate. Each legislative session day, you might be required to review the bill calendar—the list of bills that are scheduled that day for floor debate. These may include proposed legislation for which your legislator is the prime or cosponsor, as well as legislation of importance to his or her particular constituents. As an alert intern, it may very well be your responsibility to prepare your legislator for the debate and the vote.

As a capitol intern you will be at the forefront of state politics. You may have the opportunity to rub elbows with significant elected state officials and other leaders, including the governor and federal representatives. Most capitol interns report that they are thrilled to be able to see and meet elected officials who are responsible for their state's governance, including the distribution of billions of dollars in state revenues. They say they are both awed by the responsibility and invigorated by the challenge. In every sense, most capitol interns develop a new appreciation for the wide range of challenges their legislators face and of the legislative process.

The District Office Experience

Perhaps the most common response from interns who work in the district office is "I didn't realize people contact you about *everything!*" For although the range of issues that confronts the district office is often overwhelming, a legislator deems nothing impossible. Your role as an intern will be to see that every caller, visitor, or letter writer is made to feel important, assuring each that the issue will be forwarded to the legislator. If the issue is assigned to you, your task, with guidance, will be to think through the problem, figure out a plan of attack, consult your legislator, take the appropriate course of action, and follow up with the constituent. From the intern who had to deal with the woman whose children were being bitten by her neighbor's geese (a true story) to the one who needed an answer for a man who declared "there ought to be a law" against his neighbor's leaves blowing on his lawn, all questions, concerns, and suggestions are handled in the heart of the district—the district office.

Although you may certainly expect to deal with legislative and budgetary issues, particularly during the legislative session, your primary focus in the district office will be the individual constituent—the lifeblood of a legislative office. Your tasks may involve coordinating benefits and services with various state agencies; advocating on behalf of or to local municipalities or federal governmental representatives; researching pending changes to existing laws, many of them directly affecting individual lives; tracking down resources and funding opportunities for various community projects; communicating the legislator's positions on a recent vote; and writing lots and lots of letters.

When talking with us about their experiences in the district office, many interns expressed their delight and pleasure in helping individuals with their problems. Whether it was helping a mother who was not able to find health care to find aid for her chronically ill child or assisting the man who was injured on the job to get a workers' compensation administrative hearing to cover his family's living expenses, many interns develop a real sense of satisfaction and usefulness. One intern felt so emotionally involved with one family that she actually wept when resources were found to assist a woman involved in a domestic violence incident. For the elected state representative and the assisting intern, serving as an advocate is often as important as proposing a new law or passing a budget.

The Campaign Trail Experience

If your internship coincides with an election year for your state legislator, you may be asked to devote a portion of your time to the campaign office. If you like the excitement of the campaign trail and the heat of political battle, this can be an exciting and enlightening process. Of course, the campaign experience is greatly enhanced by victory!

You should expect to spend time reviewing and learning about the campaign issues as well as the candidates. Your time will be divided between stuffing envelopes with campaign literature or fundraising invitations; going door-to-door with your candidate to meet and greet voters; participating in "lit-drops," where you pass out informational brochures and literature supporting your candidate; phoning registered voters encouraging their support; and perhaps doing research to prepare your candidate for a debate or meet-the-candidate session.

On Election Day you might be expected to call voters whom your campaign has targeted for support, urging them to go to the polls. You may also be asked to arrange rides for voters, answer phones at the campaign headquarters, or visit the polls. Interns have been known to share the task of delivering cookies and candy to the poll workers on Election Day, assuring that the legislator is remembered. You will quickly learn that such little touches mean a lot in the political arena.

With any luck, when the polls close and the votes are tallied, your time and effort will be rewarded with a victory celebration. If you're like many interns we've talked to, you'll become emotionally involved in the campaign, viewing the election's outcome as a personal victory or loss. That is all part of the political game; it can also be very gratifying to know that you played a part in your state's political process.

Getting Started on the Job

Keeping Track of Your Time

Once you have reviewed and discussed with your supervisor your role as a legislative intern, you should determine the days and the number of hours you plan to work. Again, it is best to work in longer blocks of time rather than an hour here and an hour there. You want to allow for enough time to become involved in a project.

You also need to allow for callbacks from state agency personnel or another governmental office you may contact for information. Otherwise, you will always be playing phone tag and never get anything accomplished.

Because state legislators typically have small staffs, you may get an opportunity to work very closely with your legislator. You should allow yourself enough time for this to happen. Try to arrange for a block of time when your schedules overlap. Remember: always dress appropriately, just in case the legislator wants you to attend an event outside the office.

Keep a record of your own time and the number of hours you have worked both in- and outside the office. Although most offices will have some type of a designated time sheet for you to record your time, it is preferable that you take the initiative.

Dependability: Attendance and Punctuality

It goes without saying that you will be expected to show up when you are scheduled to be in the office and to be on time. Not only is this a courtesy to your legislator and the office staff, but it is also important to demonstrate that you are responsible and take your role seriously. Most office supervisors plan activities and duties for their interns, including time on the computers, of which there are often few. If you are ill or for some other reason cannot make your scheduled time, be certain to call and explain. An explanation ahead of time is far better than an excuse after the fact. Do not make a habit of arriving late. Your attendance and punctuality is a direct reflection on your attitude toward your internship and will affect your job performance review.

Learning to Take and Keep Notes

When you first begin your internship, there will be many names, places, and facts that you won't know, nor will you remember them all unless you take notes. Your notebook should become your constant companion and guide. You should begin your record keeping by writing down the important names and contact numbers for the immediate office personnel and expand that list on a daily basis. It is preferable that you write a brief summary of all your constituent contacts and the issues you are handling. You should record the names of elected community officials, from the federal government down to the village mayor, and definitely the names of those who provide you with useful information and resource material. They may prove to be useful at another time. Your notes and records of your cases will also help you in reviewing and assessing your internship, should you have to file a final class report. Do not always count on your memory to see you through.

A Little Grunt Work Can't Hurt You

Here's a good rule to remember: A state intern can expect to do no more than what a "regular" staff member is expected to do, nor should they expect to do any less! There are many unglamorous tasks no one particularly likes yet that are at the very heart of any legislative office. These tasks are often referred to affectionately as "grunt work." Although a state legislative internship can be a thrilling and ennobling opportunity, much of the basic, daily office work is routine and mundane. If you view this part of your internship as drudgery, beneath you, or boring, then you may miss some important lessons along the way.

There are certain chores that, when wisely evaluated, can be beneficial in expanding your knowledge. Newspaper clipping is one. Most legislative offices review local and statewide press clippings from daily and weekly papers. Items selected for review usually cover state and local governmental issues, current community events, and key issues of importance to the individual legislator (for example, child care, long-term care, the environment, auto insurance, property taxes). Weekly community newspapers also offer information on upcoming events of interest to the legislator, as well as names of individuals and organizations that should receive congratulatory letters for specific achievements. Interns may also be asked to check Internet news services on a daily basis, thereby expanding the available press information.

Other basic office tasks include such duties as filing, updating lists and files, answering the phones, inputting data, and processing bulk mailings. For example, you may be asked to contact all the school boards in the legislator's district to obtain an updated list of board members, or you may be asked to contact local unions to update the list of their presidents and addresses. These updated lists could prove valuable in communicating with constituents about a pressing educational or labor issue. In addition, filing letters, research material, and legislative communiqués also assists you in learning the issues and the relevant contact names.

One of the most important tasks in a legislative office is taking a good phone message. Practice using your telephone voice. Go over with your supervisor the appropriate way to answer the phone and what information you need to get from the caller. Talk slowly and distinctly. Many times, callers are either anxious or involved in their personal issues; they often jump right into *their* issues without even giving their names. It is up to you to obtain not only a name but also a return contact telephone number and an address, when possible. Get as much information as possible regarding the caller and why he or she is calling. Learn to listen carefully and allow the caller a chance to talk. Never promise that the legislator will call back; simply say that you will give the legislator the message. If you do not know the answer to the caller's question, ask the caller to hold on while you refer the call to someone who can help. You may also legitimately say that, although you do not know the answer to the question, you will attempt to find out and have someone get back to him or her. Try not to keep the caller on hold for very long. If the caller is rude or offensive, you should probably transfer the call to a staff member. Always remain polite to the caller, regardless of his or her demeanor, and be sure to inform your supervisor of such calls.

If you take a call from the press, never immediately say that the legislator is available. If you can, refer the call immediately to the appropriate staff member. If necessary, take a detailed message and make every effort to find out what issue the reporter is calling about, so that you can notify the legislator. Also inquire as to the reporter's deadline or time frame.

In most offices, daily messages are logged on a computer file as a method of cataloging complaints and issues for follow-up and review. How you take and record your message is vital to this process, as well as to establishing a positive rapport with the caller.

The Nuts and Bolts of the Legislative Office

Learning Your Role and Responsibilities

Your assignments will consist of a variety of responsibilities. Doing short-term research projects and responding to constituent mail are primary. Know at the outset, and remember throughout your internship, that your role is supportive; you are not a decision maker. You should not anticipate drafting legislation or writing position papers for the legislator. It takes time to learn the ropes and the roles, but there are steps you can take to enhance your usefulness and effectiveness.

First, know the territory: What does a state legislator do? What is the geography of the legislative district? And what is the makeup of the district politically (conservative, liberal, moderate) and socioeconomically (rural, urban, suburban). Second but equally important, acquire a basic understanding of how the legislature functions: How is a bill introduced? What is the committee structure? How does a bill come to the floor of the legislature? How does a bill become law? This information is readily available on the Internet, or your legislator can provide you reading material.

Third, learn who the "players" are in both the legislature and the district. You may very well need to consult with staff members from legislative committees, state agencies, and government at all levels (village, town, county, state, and federal).

Special Projects

There may be occasions when you will be challenged to work on a special assignment or research project, either one you've chosen or one assigned to you. Interns in general like to become involved in special projects requiring them to expand their focus. Be alert for assignments that appeal to your interests and play to your skills. Here are two examples of interns who successfully completed special assignments resulting directly from the office's dynamics.

When Brian first interviewed for his internship, he mentioned in passing that he had a real interest in writing press releases and enjoyed designing and producing graphic materials for campaigns. Although, at the time of his original interview, there was no need for another press release person, during the election campaign, the person who was going to do the press releases and design the legislator's webpage became ill and could not continue with his volunteer position. Brian was willing and able to complete the task, thereby fulfilling both his interest and the needs of the campaign.

Sarah was interning in a district office. Although she was a very capable individual, she did not like to write letters, nor was it her strong suit. However, she had experience as a telephone complaint clerk and had worked in an office setting during the summer. The district office to which she was assigned was temporarily short staffed, having lost its receptionist/scheduler. Sarah was able to step in to fill the void until a replacement was found. She not only was accomplished at the task but also enjoyed the experience.

Other interns have specifically expressed interest in special research projects on issues ranging from long-term health care (because the intern had a grandparent who required nursing home assistance) to state-supported special education funding for families with "exceptional" children (because the intern's sister was a special needs child, and her family was not able to fund a placement at a suitable facility).

Representing the Legislator

On occasion you may be called upon either to represent or accompany your legislator to a meeting or public event. In these instances especially, it is important to dress appropriately. Again, jeans, shorts, and tank tops are not appropriate. Because you may not be forewarned of an event, always come prepared to be seen and heard inside or outside the office setting.

Your Role as an Ambassador

Your legislator will be remembered by the impression you leave with constituents and the public in general. Always make sure that you introduce yourself and mention whom you are representing. In most instances, you probably will not be expected to speak publicly. For the most part, remember that you are there to represent your legislator and to take information back. If you should be asked to say a few words, it is always a safe bet to simply express the legislator's personal regret, possibly giving a reason why she or he could not attend and saying that you will be reporting to her or him.

Gathering Information

Remember that events are *working* engagements, not *social* dates. Always glean as much information as you can. It is wise to take along your notebook to record the names of those in attendance, particularly other public officials. If informational material and/or press packets are available, make sure you pick one up for your legislator's review. It also will help you in preparing a brief report on the event.

Reporting Back

Following the event or meeting, type a brief summary of what you did, whom you met, and what you learned. Your legislator may also request that you do additional research or investigate an issue further. This may require that you continue to communicate with those you met at the event. Thus your role as an ambassador may result in future meetings and additional recognition for the legislator.

Professional Ethics and Confidentiality

Just as legislators have a code of conduct to which they have sworn allegiance, so should you be willing to abide by your office's personal and professional ethics. What you see, hear, and read while in the legislative office remains within those walls. There may be times in which information that could affect someone's personal safety is reported to the legislative office. Although you may smile at the constituent who does not want his neighbor's leaves in his yard, you are equally likely to hear chilling reports of illegal drug activity, domestic violence, child abuse, sexual harassment, job discrimination, and medical malpractice. You have not only the responsibility but also the obligation to refrain from discussing constituent issues outside the office.

Likewise, information related to pending legislation, including funding, may not always be for immediate public consumption. Everyone wants to feel important, and having special knowledge is often the way to make yourself appear important. Although your legislator will often advise you if something is highly confidential, your best rule of thumb is to avoid talking about the specifics of your internship outside the office. A line from the television series *The West Wing* highlights this point: "Those who speak don't know, and those who know don't speak." You would do well to heed this advice.

If you would like to keep copies of the response letters or research papers you have written, always ask permission to make copies. You may be required to block out the names of individuals or companies. Also, it is advisable that you check before removing any folders or computer files from the office. There is always risk of the office losing important documentation.

Finally, there is also something to be said for loyalty to your legislator that should continue well after you complete your internship. Although you will, no doubt, be free to talk about your experience, negativism has a way of wending its way back to the legislator and could well come back to influence your future employment opportunities.

Being and Feeling a Part of the Team

Because you will not be working in a vacuum, it is important that you build relationships with the existing legislative office staff. Although you do not have to become "buddies," you should communicate on a regular basis about what projects you have been assigned and how you are progressing. Usually your supervisor or, possibly, your legislator will assign you a project. If you do not understand an assignment, feel free to ask questions; do not wait until your deadline passes and the assignment is not finished.

Be open to your supervisor's feedback. Remember that no one wants you to fail, since failure is almost always a direct reflection on the quality of the instruction. If you disagree with your assessment, an assignment, or a task, by all means talk with your supervisor or other office personnel first, prior to meeting with your legislator.

Having Fun

Take your job seriously but remember also to have fun. Although you are expected to be professional in your demeanor and thorough in your work responsibilities, certainly most legislators also want the experience to be enjoyable. Legislators want you to be excited about their profession, getting a taste and feel for the political world to which they have devoted so much of their time and attention. They want you to be excited about rubbing elbows with leading governmental decision makers; they want you to experience the challenges of real politics.

Try to find the humor in the experience. Dealing with constituents, government agencies, and elected officials is often both humorous and heartwarming. Why do you think politics is the subject of so many cartoons?

Saying Goodbye

Like all good things—and it is hoped that your internship will be a good experience—it must come to an end. How you deal with your last few days on the job could affect your career choice and future job opportunities. So here are a few tips that might, hopefully, smooth your transition out of the office.

Leave on Good Terms

No one wants to leave a position with negative feelings—not only about those with whom you have worked but also about your experience. During your final week make sure that you continue to be punctual and follow through on all your outstanding assignments. If you are not able to complete an assigned task or if you have not as yet received a response, by all means tell your legislator, supervisor, or another staff member.

If you have any outstanding issues for which you feel uncomfortable, ask to discuss them with the state legislator. It is better to clear the air than to harbor feelings of resentment, doubt, or misunderstanding. After all, you want to keep them begging for more rather than holding your coat at the door.

Ask for a Letter of Reference

If you feel that you have done an acceptable job, by all means ask for a general letter of reference. Although you may wait until you are applying for a specific educational or employment opportunity, writing the letter while the memory of you is fresh generally results in a stronger, more personalized recommendation.

Remember to Say Thank You

During the first week following the completion of your internship, take the time to write a thank-you note. Specifically, remember to highlight those things about your internship that you found to be most beneficial. Remember that legislators also need to receive feedback on how well they perform their jobs. Down the road, give a call or stop by the office occasionally. You never know when you might need a reference, a kind word, or friend in the world of politics.

8

Internships with
Nonprofit Organizations

Joanne Tait
Sierra Club

Anonprofit organization is a corporation organized for public
benefit, not for anyone's private gain, so its office probably
won't have the plush facilities its detractors may depict. If you
choose to work for a nonprofit organization after your internship,
you probably won't receive the perks, benefits, and wealth you may
receive at larger for-profit corporations, but you will get to work
on issues you care deeply about and make a difference where it's
needed most. So if it's a sense of personal fulfillment connected to
a broader purpose that you're most looking for in an internship experience, in addition of course to acquiring marketable professional skills, the nonprofit political organization may be the ideal
internship for you.

Office Organization

My office, the Sierra Club's headquarters in Washington, D.C., is
typical of many nonprofits. It is composed of three brick, three-
story row houses, which can be somewhat of a maze to newcomers.
Many staff members have their own offices, others share office
space, and still others are located in corners with desks. Interns
may be situated in an open area, at a makeshift desk, or if they're
lucky, at a real desk in close proximity to those they work with.

Types of Work Done in Nonprofit Organizations

Nonprofit organizations deal with a wide range of issues. The tax codes and other laws of the Internal Revenue Service (IRS) govern the kinds of work a nonprofit organization can do. Many organizations hold a section 501(c)(3) status, which allows them to do charitable, educational, and public outreach work to promote their issues and mission. These organizations typically are not allowed to participate in electoral politics, or have very limited resources they can allocate toward directly influencing elected officials, public policy, or legislation. Most of these organizations' work is performed to raise public awareness and promote their issues. They may conduct research or perform a study and release the results to the public. They may create fact sheets or issue reports to increase public knowledge and awareness of the organization and its goals. They will then use various means to broadcast information promoting their cause to the people they think will become interested in their issues or will in turn want to promote the issues and mission of the organization to others.

The Sierra Club falls into a second tax code category established by the IRS: It is a 501(c)(4) organization. The work these organizations engage in may include, but is not limited to, direct lobbying of elected officials for the intent of affecting public policy and legislation. 501(c)(4) organizations have more flexibility to attempt to influence legislation that has an impact on the organization's goals and mission. They may also encourage their membership to contact elected officials for the express purpose of influencing legislation, a form of indirect lobbying. Memberships in and donations made to a 501(c)(3) organization are tax-deductible contributions, while memberships in and donations made to a 501(c)(4) organization are not, primarily due to their ability to influence elected officials and public policy.

Both types of nonprofit organizations may utilize different vehicles, strategies, or tactics to get their messages out to the public. The use of polling information to gauge what the general public thinks about a particular issue is one useful tool. These polling results may suggest that a particular issue being tested is not significantly important to the general public at that time. Given the fact that politics is ever changing and dynamic, the organization's issue may not be on the general public's radar screen. Should this be the case, and it often is, the organization may not wish to invest its limited resources for print, radio, or television ads (expensive communication tools). The organization may elect to wait until its issues again come to the forefront of public opinion before spending its hard-earned funds to draw more attention to the issues. Essentially, the organization gets more bang for its buck when the issues are of greater importance to the general public. Polling information may also be used to help formulate the message that will be sent out to the public and is usually crafted by a media or communications department within the organization. Polls may also help to determine the best spin or angle to put on an issue so that it will be better received.

Another strategy that nonprofit organizations may employ for getting the word out is free or "earned" media. Earned media may be in the form of letters to the editor or opinion editorials. Letters in rebuttal or support on the issues may also be written to local or national news outlets in response to articles that a newspaper has recently printed. Free media may create a buzz for the organization's issues and is a vital tool used by many nonprofits. Another form of earned media is the press conference. Depending on the level of media coverage, press conferences can be a valuable resource used to garner attention to the nonprofit's mission. An additional media tool is the press release—a statement made by the organization that shows where it stands on a particular action or issue directly affecting some aspect of the organization. Press releases are an effective way of keeping the press and public abreast of the group's positions and mission.

Other crucial work done in a nonprofit organization includes research, development, and grassroots organizing. When an organization is planning to release a report on a particular issue, it conducts research and gathers information to produce a fact sheet highlighting one or more of the issues. Fact sheets are valuable tools that provide concise factual information selected and presented to attract public attention to important facets of the issues. They are also fairly inexpensive to produce and can be handed out at "tabling events," conferences or other highly visible activities where organizations set up tables for distributing information, getting signatures for a petition or post card, and/or recruiting members. This work done outside the office not only is fun but also leads to another centrally important aspect of the work done by many nonprofits: organizing and grassroots (citizen-activist) outreach. Organizing public participation plays a vital role for most nonprofits and is often the backbone that keeps the movement together. There is normally a direct correlation between the level of grassroots support and the organization's effectiveness. Volunteers and grassroots activists are also regular voters. If the voters don't agree with the viewpoints and decisions of their officials, they may vote for someone else come election time. The voting public often follows the cues of their favorite nonprofits in deciding how to vote.

Attending congressional hearings or going to congressional offices to lobby elected officials is another large part of the nonprofit's business. Staff may make phone calls or speak with staff members in congressional offices to see how certain members feel about their issues or may vote on a piece of legislation. A lot of work goes into these efforts: researching legislation, making phone calls to offices, sending out action alerts via email, organizing the group's members to contact their members of Congress, working with other organizations that have the same concerns, and holding press conferences. The group may draft and drop a letter to specific congressional offices urging them to take its side on a particular issue. Another type of work nonprofits may engage in is coalition building, teaming up with other like-minded organizations to establish a community of organizations having similar agendas. Although these different organizations often may not completely agree on the specifics of an issue, they become more effective as a community if they can show some solidarity on the general importance of an issue. The more agreement within a community, the more likely that message and agenda will move forward.

Basic Expectations for Interns

Interns provide nonprofit organizations an extremely valuable resource they would otherwise not have: more people power to do the things that might not otherwise get done. In return, interns gain valuable, real-world experience and insights they may not get in the classroom. At any nonprofit organization, you should expect your contributions to be of great assistance and importance, and that it is a privilege for the organization to have you help them promote and carry out their goals and mission. You are an essential resource! You should keep in mind that generally all internships include the kind of work that you'd probably rather not do and that staffers don't have time to do. You may be expected to do filing, photocopying, and other routine tasks; but these are not the only things you'll do. These seemingly simple tasks will provide you with valuable opportunities to get a basic understanding of the organization, its structure, inner workings, and goals, and serve as a good introduction before you begin to tackle more substantive work. It's not so much what you do that matters as how you approach completing any assignment.

Again, there are a wide variety of things you can expect to do as an intern with a nonprofit. It will of course depend on the organization, whether it has a 501(c)(3) or 501(c)(4) status, the type of internship you choose, and your willingness to be involved and contribute.

As an intern assigned to the media group of a nonprofit, for example, you may expect to write materials for press releases, organize press conferences, draft talking points, write opinion editorials, or maintain databases for communication purposes.

If you work in the legislative area you may be expected to conduct research for a particular report the organization is pulling together. There are many research tools you may use, such as the Internet, publications or studies conducted by other organizations, previous reports published by your nonprofit, newspapers, journals, and many other resources. You may draft fact sheets or update website information and volunteer databases. You may be asked to write articles for newsletters that your organization publishes for its members. You may be asked to participate at tabling events. With organizations such as the Sierra Club, you may accompany staff on lobbying visits to congressional offices or attend congressional hearings on issues the organization is tracking. If your office is in Washington or a state capital, you may be expected to participate in "Hill drops"—taking letters to targeted congressional or legislative offices. The targeted officials are those whom the organization thinks it may influence by urging them to vote one way or another on a particular piece of legislation. You may also be asked to attend and take notes at coalition meetings or legislative hearings and to brief your supervisor afterwards.

As an intern at a nonprofit working in the political arena, you may do many of the same things as interns working in other branches of the organization. You may participate in election activities, including candidate endorsements, fundraisers, and literature distributions.

Being a Professional in the Nonprofit Environment

As an intern, to be a professional in the nonprofit sector, you should pay attention to the way other office staff conduct themselves and align your behavior accordingly. The Sierra Club has a relatively casual work environment but maintains a very professional work ethic. In general you'll be expected to put in the normal hours of a full-time staff member, and to get the most out of your internship experience, you will need to put in the hours and hard work that other staffers do. Again, this may vary depending on the current events and work that needs to be done that week. Some weeks may be longer if there are events or congressional happenings that need to be addressed. Deadlines for getting out reports or information may also be cause to put in a few extra hours above and beyond the normal workweek. Be willing to work overtime.

Keys to Getting Substantive Work

There is always work to be done, no matter how slow or uneventful things may seem at a given time. To get substantive projects to work on, you should exhibit interest and enthusiasm in all that you do, even if it's not a project you like. It's important to realize that doing the routine tasks completely and correctly will help improve your future opportunities. The more you function as a team player, the more appreciated your efforts will be and, in turn, the more responsibility you'll be given. Once you are viewed as genuinely interested and enthusiastic, good things will come your way.

As an intern with little or no work experience, you may find it difficult being thrown into an office environment. It's good to show interest and take initiative, even if you're unsure of yourself. Don't be afraid to ask questions! Staff members understand that you may not know everything, and that's okay. The more you get involved and ask questions, the more you'll learn and be able to take on additional responsibilities and substantive work.

Another way for you to get more involved and get varied assignments is to offer your opinions and suggestions. Sometimes staff members who have been working for an organization for a long time get so wrapped up in it that they may lose their objectivity and ability to approach topics from a fresh perspective. It's often helpful to get views from young interns just entering the field. After all, you are these organizations' future.

Another important thing to keep in mind is to have a positive attitude and a sense of humor in approaching your work. Supervisors will generally recognize your enthusiasm and be more inclined to give you more substantial projects.

It's also helpful for you to have specific goals that you wish to accomplish during your internship. What do you want to get out of your internship? Write down these goals and share them with your supervisor at the beginning of the internship; he or she will more than likely be willing to help you accomplish them. If you're interning simply to get credit for a required class and you come to the internship with a lackadaisical attitude, you're not likely to get anything valuable from your experience. The relationship between interns and nonprofit organizations is one that should be mutually beneficial. The more you put into it, the more you will get out of it. It's up to you.

Mannerisms, Culture, and Mores

How to Dress for Your Internship

When you come to work as an intern, a good rule of thumb is to observe how other members of the office conduct themselves. What to wear may depend on what the day has in store for you. If you're going to a congressional hearing, you would dress in business attire. If you don't have to go to any meetings or public events, you may be able to dress more casually, as the office atmosphere dictates. The Sierra Club is pretty casual; typically people wear khakis or even jeans. Shorts in the summertime are not an unusual sight. If you've got a meeting on Capitol Hill, however, you must dress appropriately. Also, if you are attending other meetings or press events and you are going as a representative of your organization, you will want to dress in a professional and appropriate manner. You should always check with your supervisor if you are unsure, especially when you are representing the organization.

Language

Another challenge that may arise during your internship is making sense of office lingo and political jargon. Many times acronyms get thrown about and you may have no clue what they mean. To use the Sierra Club again as an example, when the organization hired a new deputy political director, a fairly high-level position, she came to the office and began to get involved with conference calls and meetings, and the acronym *ESA* was constantly being used. Coming from a political and not an environmental background, she had no idea what this stood for, so finally she asked and learned that it stands for the Endangered Species Act. This is one of those situations where you take it for granted, when you've been working in a particular field for a while, that everyone knows what you're talking about, yet even a senior-level person may not know what is being said. Once you figure out the office lingo, it makes your job or internship a lot easier to understand!

Many organizations, including the Sierra Club, have a list of commonly used acronyms that they will provide you with, and you should try to familiarize yourself with the terms. Of course, they are not all going to be listed, so if you don't know, ask! In a political climate, which many of you obviously want to enter since you're reading this book, there are many terms and much language with which you may not be familiar. If you don't have a background in political science, for example, you may find following the actions of Congress a bit challenging. The use of parliamentary rules and language, if you've never been exposed to them, may sound like Greek to you! At the start of your internship, familiarizing yourself with the language and lingo of the organization will make things a lot easier.

Ways to Have Fun

There are many ways to have a good time during your internship experience. Often there will be other interns you will work with and get to know and, since you've chosen an internship at the same organization, you've already got a lot in common. The Sierra Club, for instance, promotes a lot of fun outdoor activities outside the office. During the summer, organizations may host events such as brown bag lunches that offer the opportunity to expand your knowledge beyond that of your specific duties. Go to them when you can. You may also meet with interns from other organizations that stage events of interest to you. Local universities and dormitories may sponsor activities for interns around the area. If your internship is located in the Washington, D.C., area there is plenty to do and see. There are many restaurants, parks, and shops. The national mall has a host of museums and monuments to explore, and one of the Washington area's advantages is that the majority of these things are free—a great benefit for interns on a limited budget.

Publications and Information

It's important for your internship experience that you be informed about the issues affecting your organization. One way to keep abreast of current events is to read relevant publications. The Sierra Club, for example, uses several different publications to keep on top of the issues. Sierra Club interns might read the *Environment and Energy Daily* news bulletin to track environmental congressional news; the *Greenwire*, which is part of an online service addressing current environmental issues happening at federal, state, and local levels; and *Roll Call* and *The Hill*, newspapers devoted entirely to happenings and developments on Capitol Hill. *Congress Daily* provides information on upcoming votes, hearings, and committee actions that may be of importance to your organization. You should also read all publications that your organization publishes. The Sierra Club publishes a magazine called *Sierra* as well as an activist newsletter called the *Planet* to keep you up-to-date on happenings within the organization. Basically, any publications your organization subscribes to that affect the work you do as an intern are good resources to keep yourself in the loop.

Outside Events

There are also a lot of fun and exciting events you may attend as an intern working for a nonprofit organization. Press conferences are always great opportunities to see notable people who are important in your organization's areas of concern. Members of Congress or celebrities who are advocates for your organization's work may speak at these events. The Sierra Club has a political action committee (PAC) that allows the group to make political contributions in elections. There may be fundraisers for members of Congress that your organization has endorsed, and many times interns are welcome to attend. You may go to coalition events featuring speakers from within or outside your organization addressing important issues or celebrating community achievements. One event the Sierra Club was part of at the Clinton White House was then Secretary of the Interior Bruce Babbitt's farewell address, in which he reviewed his achievements in the environmental movement. Several of our interns were able to attend this exciting event.

Dealings with the Outside World

When you work as an intern, you are acting as a representative, and the manner in which you conduct yourself is a direct reflection on the organization. You should keep this fact in mind particularly when dealing with those outside the organization.

Volunteers

Working with nonprofits usually involves working with volunteers. Sometimes this can be a bit delicate. The volunteers devote their time and effort to helping your organization and are not paid for it—something you can relate to as an intern in most cases. Volunteers may have their own ideas of what they want to be doing, which is reasonable and often does not pose a problem. Sometimes, however, the volunteers have their own agenda that does not agree with the organization's established policies. If a volunteer is doing something you know is not in compliance with the organization, you should notify your supervisor immediately. Sometimes the situation may be remedied very easily, but it usually requires tact and skill from an experienced staff member to reach an agreeable resolution.

Lobbyists

You may also encounter lobbyists through your internship. The Sierra Club has several lobbyists on their staff. Lobbyists promote their ideas and agendas to members of Congress. When communicating with lobbyists, who are perhaps consultants for your organization, you want to make sure your message is clear and concise. It is important to arm them with facts and information that will support your message and to offer counterarguments to any of their concerns. It is essential to be as careful and accurate as possible and never mislead them. If you don't know something, say so. Don't try to fake knowledge.

Members of Congress

When writing to members of Congress there are a few guidelines you should follow. Keep the letter short and to the point; one page is always a good length to set for your correspondence. Make sure you state your purpose for the letter in the beginning and, if it pertains to specific legislation, you should include the bill number. Always be respectful and include specific information to support your argument. The letter should be addressed appropriately as well: "The Honorable [full name of member]," followed by the address. In the salutation your letter should read, "Dear Senator or Representative," with his or her last name. If you are meeting face-to-face with a member of Congress, you should be respectful, courteous, and professional. Keep in mind that when you meet these members at their offices or at a function or event for your organization, you are a direct reflection on your organization. You don't want to make the wrong impression and damage your organization's reputation.

Professional Staff in Other Offices

Basically the same rules apply when dealing with other professionals outside your organization. You want to be professional, respectful, and courteous to those you encounter. If someone does not treat you with the same level of respect, that isn't a reason for you to be disrespectful in return. You should always walk the higher ground should you ever encounter such a situation and speak to a supervisor if you feel you can't handle a negative situation.

Other Political Parties

Generally many nonprofit organizations operate in a bipartisan manner. This means that they do not side with either of the two main parties (Democrats or Republicans) on issues but rather work to gain support from both sides of the aisle. Always keep in mind that many issues may cross party lines, and that is something to take advantage of. When a bill finally passes both House and Senate and becomes law, it almost always has supporters from both parties behind it. Again, being respectful and open to other people's viewpoints is usually the best way to go.

If, however, your organization is usually affiliated with a particular political party, it is still in the organization's best interest to have good relations with the other party. The more broadly the organization's reach extends among members of the public, the more effective the organization will be. It is usually counterproductive for an organization to alienate large groups of constituents—a good reason to keep communication lines open and in good standing.

The Most Important Things to Do
and Not Do as an Intern

You may one day be able to look back on your internship as a launching ground for your future endeavors. No matter what career path you choose, your internship can be a great way to make a smooth transition from life at school to life in the work world. There are so many things you can do as an intern to make your experience memorable and valuable.

One former intern at the Sierra Club provides a great example. Jessica was always willing to help out, no matter what the task. She took initiative in finding things that needed to be done, and she did them. She never complained about making photocopies or doing other seemingly mundane things that always must be done but instead approached everything with a professional and enthusiastic attitude. She also had a great sense of humor and approached all she did with a smile. In turn, she got the recognition by her supervisor, who saw what a capable person she was and gave her more substantive work. She then conducted research for one of the Sierra Club's priority campaigns and drafted fact sheets. She proposed a new approach for updating fact sheets, and her idea was welcomed. She was also assigned to write opinion editorials and articles for a newsletter and given the responsibility of updating the website and activist databases.

Another great quality Jessica had was attention to detail. She was always double-checking her work to make sure it was accurate and thoroughly researched before handing it to her supervisor for review. The attitude and accuracy of Jessica's work was something her supervisor noticed. When later asked to write letters of recommendation, the supervisor was happy to do so and remembered all the little things that made Jessica such a standout. She was always willing to pitch in and help whenever needed. She made it a point to ask questions and get involved with the organization's work. She put in the extra hours when schedules were tight and a campaign was on deadline. When times are tight, the more hands available, the quicker the project will get done—and your hard work will definitely be noticed.

There are also things you should *not do* as an intern. Another example comes to mind of an intern—I won't provide his name—who ended up being rather problematic, and his experience was unpleasant both for him and the organization. He was not always willing to help out when asked, saying he was too busy with other things—unfortunately those things were not related to his internship or even to the organization. This is not something you should do if you want to gain experience and excel in your internship. Another bad decision by the intern was his unwillingness to participate in Hill drops on a particular day. These are very important letters to members of Congress, and you certainly don't want to come off as if you are too important or can't be bothered to help if you want to establish a good reputation. Needless to say, this intern was not able to generate a good letter of recommendation.

Make sure you get plenty of rest during your nonwork hours! One of our past interns was given an assignment; when someone went to check on her progress, she was found napping at the desk! This particular intern was often found talking on the phone to her friends. It's one thing to make a brief, local personal call from time to time, but when your supervisor is constantly interrupting you while you're talking to friends, you make a bad impression. And remember, you are interning at a nonprofit organization, so the staff do not appreciate you spending their limited resources on personal, long-distance calls. Ask before you dial, or use your calling card.

Sometimes successful interns may go on to get permanent jobs at the organization. In fact, several current employees at the Sierra Club are former interns. It's great for the organization to hire someone who is already familiar with its purpose and structure and great for the intern to experience something they would like to pursue as a career. You may be excited about an organization, however, only to find that when you do the actual work, it's not something you want to pursue. Either way, your internship can help you sort through your options and provide a basis for future endeavors.

Conducting Research

9

Congressional Research

R. Eric Petersen
CONGRESSIONAL RESEARCH SERVICE

For several weeks, the newspapers and television networks have been all over the story. A large company, much heralded for its innovative business practices, big profits, and muscular political activity, has imploded in a spectacular bankruptcy. As if the negative national effects on market confidence and general economic outlook weren't enough, most of the company's operations are located in the congressional district of the member of Congress who selected you for an internship. It is your first week in the office. Although most of your formal training is yet to come, you have already been asked to look into the details of bankruptcy law, track the company's campaign contributions, determine which company officers made millions while laying off thousands, and learn which federal programs can offer financial and educational assistance to a large number of suddenly unemployed workers back in the district. This information will be used to shape your member's legislative, representational, and political responses to this home-based national event.

Welcome to Capitol Hill. Good thing you arrived during a slow week.

Members of Congress need a wide range of information to carry out the legislative, representational, and oversight responsibilities of their offices. They depend, to a large degree, on their staff—and their interns—to gather the information and data that they need to do their job.

In legislative matters, the member may need information about pending legislation or analysis to develop his or her understanding of a complex set of competing policy proposals. In representational work, members put a premium on service as part of their representational role as a facilitator and liaison between their constituents and the national government. During your internship, you may be asked to gather information to answer constituent inquiries or evaluate polling data to determine what constituents in the home district or state are thinking. Oversight work may require an intern to delve into the intricacies of a wide variety of public programs. As with the case of the crumbling company back in the district, you may find that your research encompasses all three areas. All of this activity is carried out in a political environment characterized by intense pressure, tight deadlines, and intense competition for time and member attention.

Your internship will be successful if you improve your existing skills and develop new skills to draw from a wide range of information sources. By improving your research skills, you will be able to respond quickly and accurately to a variety of information requests.

This chapter discusses the skills an individual should bring to a congressional internship, as well as offering a broad overview of resources available for conducting research in support of the legislative, representational, and oversight activities in congressional offices.

Research Skills

The type and scope of the research performed in a congressional office depend in large part on members' needs and how the research will be used. A broad set of skills and abilities will serve you well as you take on your first assignments. Some of these skills and abilities are minimum qualifications to get the internship; don't worry if you don't think you have all of them. If you have successfully made it through one or two semesters of college, you have already demonstrated these skills, and they will be developed and strengthened during the internship experience. They include:

- a willingness to learn;
- curiosity and inventiveness;
- an ability to work under sometimes stressful conditions;

- basic research skills, including identifying information sources and searching computer databases;
- good written and oral communication skills; and
- an ability to manage your time so you can set deadlines for work to be completed and meet deadlines set by others.

These skills and abilities will improve and be complemented by other skills that will emerge through your on-the-job experience. Valuable research skills that can be gained in a congressional internship include:

- an ability to find and develop appropriate sources of information;
- a capacity to deploy evidence rather than assertion in support of policy positions;
- objectivity in gathering and evaluating information;
- insight into the strengths and weaknesses of arguments advanced by policy advocates of wide-ranging preferences and points of view;
- the ability to make clear, concise presentations both orally and in writing; and
- a grasp of the member's standards, preferences, and constituency.

As the new skills merge with the better-honed older skills, you will become more valuable as an intern in your congressional office. At the end of the experience you will have an improved set of skills and abilities that you can use as you continue your education or undertake further internship and career opportunities.

Producing Effective Research

There is no one right way to conduct congressional research, but you will be able to more effectively focus your research if you know the purpose of the research, how the information you find will be used, and how your member or supervisor wants the information you developed presented. You can achieve this by approaching your work according to four broad guidelines:

- Define the breadth of the research effort. What questions does the member or your supervisor want answered? At the beginning of the process, ask for as much information about the assignment as you can. Speak to him or her early and often as the project unfolds to define the scope of the research and what is expected of you.
- You must have a clear research strategy. What information is needed to answer the questions? Is the information available? How will it be collected? For what will it be used?
- Collect the information. A range of sources, from books to periodicals, press releases, government reports, and databases, may be consulted, collected, and organized into a coherent, workable body of information.
- Present the information. This may take the form of raw data for a larger project, a press release, or a letter you draft to a constituent.

With these basic guidelines, you will be able to conduct research in a range of areas of interest in a congressional office. Although the guidelines can be summarized, the process of research is never as simple as it seems. You should not be surprised when you discover new information that changes the way you look at your work and requires you to change part of your research strategy. At other times, you may find that the information you need is not available. In these situations, it is important for you to be flexible, to maintain your curiosity and sense of humor, and to have planned your work so as to allow time for these occurrences.

Sources and Resources for Research

In a congressional office, the most precious resource is usually time. Dozens of projects and hundreds of issues vie for member and staff time. In many cases, the research you are asked to carry out will have already been completed by an agency of the government, journalists, or scholars, so it is seldom necessary to start from scratch. Your contribution to the success of a congressional office will be multiplied if you can find and use what is already prepared and know where to go to draw upon specialized, in-depth knowledge. There are several everyday resources with which every congressional intern needs to be familiar. As you are given specific tasks or responsibilities for legislative, representational, and oversight work, you will want to take advantage of the wide range of resources that support the congressional offices in these endeavors.

Everyday Resources

There are several resources you should consult on a daily basis throughout your congressional internship experience. These resources are easily available and often serve as good starting points for congressional research. To begin, be sure you know what everyone else on Capitol Hill knows by reading *National Journal's Congress Daily* and *Congress Daily AM* or *CQ Daily Monitor* and *CQ Weekly*, which provide daily schedules, information on congressional hearings, and discussions of pending legislation (see Box 9.1). Two weekly newspapers, *Roll Call* (available online at http://www.rollcall.com), published on Tuesday and Thursday, and *The Hill* (at http://www.thehill.com), published on Wednesday, provide exclusive coverage of Congress. The websites of each publication are updated daily with new information.

BOX 9.1 The *Congressional Quarterly.*

Whether you want to look into the issues you might address during your Capitol Hill internship or need to understand lawmaking as part of your college studies, several useful resources for learning about Congress can be found in the publications of *Congressional Quarterly* (CQ) (http://www.cq.com). Nonpartisan and independent, CQ produces a range of publications that explain current issues before Congress, identify the members and staff who make the institution run, and summarize the decisions they have made. In developing your own research, you can use CQ articles on a full array of policy topics to bring you up to speed on a new issue. Several products are available including a daily edition, weekly edition, and a research overview.

BOX 9.1   The *Congressional Quarterly*. (continued)

CQ Daily Monitor provides daily Hill schedules, committee witness lists, and bill descriptions. In addition, the *Monitor* provides a summary of all the previous day's Hill news, as well as coverage of the major players in both chambers.

CQ Weekly tracks committee activity and bill status and provides side-by-side comparisons of competing versions of bills. The weekly edition also contains details of the previous week's House and Senate votes, including information on how each representative or senator voted on a legislative measure.

Finally, the *CQ Researcher* provides detailed research and analysis into a range of public policy issues before Congress. This coverage includes a comprehensive review of the conflicts surrounding an issue, background discussion of the issue's emergence, and previous efforts to develop legislative responses. Unlike some of the people and agencies that offer you information that gives themselves a competitive advantage, CQ strives to be balanced and objective in its coverage. Although CQ should not be the only resource you examine in your research, at the very least it can assist you in organizing your thoughts and developing a framework for your research.

In each chamber of Congress, officers of each body, including the clerk of the House or secretary of the Senate and the parliamentarians of each chamber, maintain extensive operations to provide information regarding the activities they are responsible for, including scheduling and matters pending before each chamber.

Similarly, the two major political parties have several organizations that are often sources of useful information for the congressional researcher. They are especially informative on the party's position on issues before Congress. Many of these organizations provide daily or weekly updates about pending issues of interest to their party's members by fax, webpage, and email. Early in your congressional internship you may want to identify and explore the resources that are available and subscribe to those that are appropriate to the work you will be doing.

Legislative Research Resources

Because Congress writes laws, the most abundant research resources are those that directly support the lawmaking process. A wide range of electronic and print resources provide the rules and procedures of each chamber; information for tracking bills through the legislative process, including the status of particular initiatives; and the positions of those who support or oppose legislative proposals. (See Box 9.2.)

BOX 9.2 The *Congressional Record*.

The *Congressional Record* is your first resource for official information about the chamber activities of Congress. A daily compilation of the debates, speeches, and other actions on the floors of the House of Representatives and Senate, the *Record* is published every day the House or Senate is in session. The *Record* offers transcripts of the previous day's proceedings in the House and Senate, a section entitled "Extensions of Remarks" that contains material not part of spoken floor proceedings, and the "Daily Digest," which summarizes the times of meetings of both houses, legislative measures reported to the House and Senate for further consideration, and measures considered in each chamber or signed into law.

Although the *Record* does not contain the details of committee activity, it provides the time and location of committee and subcommittee meetings scheduled for the day the *Record* is printed. The Senate and House portions of the *Record* list measures reported out of their committees and thus ready for floor consideration.

In addition to the transcripts of proceedings, the House and Senate sections of the *Record* feature lists of measures introduced, including original sponsors and the committees to which they were referred. In the same sections you will find appointees to conference committees, messages from the House and Senate to each other,

---

BOX 9.2   The *Congressional Record*. (continued)

---

presidential messages and other executive branch communications to Congress, and messages from state and local governments calling for congressional actions. The Senate section also contains the names of senators filing cloture motions to end filibusters, votes on cloture motions, and notices of hearings, as well as report and vote information on treaties and nominations from the Senate's Executive Calendar.

The *Record* is distributed every day to Capitol Hill offices and libraries nationwide. A searchable electronic version with coverage from 1995 onward is available online through the Government Printing Office (GPO) at http://www.access.gpo.gov. At the conclusion of each two-year Congress, a permanent version of the *Record* is compiled on CD-ROM.

How a Bill Becomes a Law.   Useful overviews of the legislative process can be found on the official House and Senate websites, http://www.house.gov and http://www.senate.gov. The Library of Congress makes available more detailed primers on the legislative process, including *Enactment of a Law: Procedural Steps in the Legislative Process* by Robert Dove and *How Our Laws Are Made* by Charles Johnson. Johnson's booklet outlines the stages of the legislative process for the general reader and explains how to use the various publications that track that process. Both of these documents are available on the Library of Congress website, http://thomas.loc.gov.

The Senate Manual.   The *Senate Manual* contains the standing rules, orders, laws, and resolutions affecting the Senate, as well as copies of historical U.S. documents and selected statistics on the Senate and other government entities. Copies are distributed to each Senate office. The manual's "Standing Rules of the Senate" section is available in full text at http://rules.senate.gov/senaterules/menu.htm.

Jefferson's Manual.   In the House of Representatives, *Constitution, Jefferson's Manual, and Rules of the House of Representatives* is prepared for each Congress by the parliamentarian of the House and is issued as a House document. It contains the text of the Constitution, the rules of the House, and the portions of the *Manual of Parliamentary Practice*, written by Thomas Jefferson when he was vice president, that are currently pertinent to House procedure. It also includes other statutory provisions that operate as procedural rules in the House. Every congressional office should have a copy. The "Rules of the House of Representatives" section of *Jefferson's Manual* is available in full text on the website of the House rules committee at http://www.house.gov/rules/house_rules_text.htm.

Legislative Information System (LIS).   Much of the legislative process can be monitored through the Legislative Information System (LIS). LIS is an extensive collection of linked databases that is designed to provide members of Congress and their staff with access to the most current and comprehensive legislative information. It is available *only* to House and Senate offices and the legislative support agencies that serve Congress. The information available through this system comes from a variety of sources, such as government agencies, the House and Senate, commercial sources, and the Library of Congress.

During your internship, you can use LIS to retrieve schedule information for the Senate and House floor, committees, and leadership. The system also provides links to commercial news and information sources and electronic publications. Other sections of LIS provide you access to congressional committee activity, including the full text of committee reports; selected prints, hearings, and committee transcripts; committee schedules; and links to committee home pages (see Box 9.3). Additionally, there are links to each chamber's public websites (addresses listed earlier), which contain, among other resources, Senate and House member lists and links to member home pages.

Outside Interest Groups and Congressional Caucuses.   The information provided through LIS and other Congress-wide resources tends to be broad and generic. In some cases, you may need more narrowly focused information, which is available from

BOX 9.3 Committee publications.

Much of the work of Congress is carried out by committees. House and Senate committees produce a range of publications detailing their work on legislative issues, investigations, oversight, and other public policy issues. In your internship you will likely use these publications to gain an understanding of policy issues or legislation before a committee or to learn the intent of the committee as it developed particular legislation. In general, congressional committees produce transcripts of hearings, several types of reports, and calendars detailing their activities. As an intern you are likely to use committee hearings and legislative reports more than other committee publications.

Hearings

Printed and Web-based hearing documents contain the edited transcripts of testimony given during committee legislative, investigative, or oversight hearings. These documents include committee members' questions and witness responses; prepared statements by committee members, witnesses, and other interested parties; and supporting documents submitted to the committee.

Legislative Reports

Committees issue several types of reports, including those that accompany a legislative measure when it is reported for chamber consideration, reports on oversight or investigative activities, and reports of conference committees. Most reports accompany legislation. Under House rules every legislative measure sent from committee to the House must be accompanied by a written report. The Senate does not require written committee reports, but they are sometimes prepared. These reports provide an explanation of a measure, the committee's actions in considering it, and arguments why the House or Senate should approve the committee's position on the bill or legislative matter. Under the rules of both chambers, reports must allow for minority, supplemental, and additional views of committee members.

You will often find in a report explanations of the committee's intent in developing the legislation, as well as why the proposal offered

---

BOX 9.3 Committee publications. (continued)

---

was chosen over other policy alternatives. Executive branch agencies routinely turn to committee reports when developing rules and regulations to implement a new law. The courts turn to the reports to discover legislative intent when a law is challenged on legal or constitutional grounds.

---

several sources. Within Congress, various congressional caucuses, coalitions, ad hoc task forces, and other informal groups can provide information on legislative issues pertaining to their membership. Examples of these groups include, among others, the Congressional Black Caucus, the Missile Defense Caucus, the Anti-Poverty Task Force, the Education Caucus, and the Environmental Task Force.

Outside resources, including interest groups, think tanks, industry representatives, labor unions, professional associations, and other organizations can be important sources of information for legislative research on issues that have an impact on their organization or their membership.

Representational and Oversight Research

Whereas legislative research in a congressional office exposes you to legislative proposals that are under consideration, representational and oversight research will take you into areas where a law has been passed and a public program has been established. Representational research involves constituent casework and other activities that demonstrate your member's commitment to serving the people of his or her district or state. Oversight research examines the implementation of government programs and policies by executive branch agencies.

Representational research focuses on the district or state and is dedicated in part to raising your member's profile among the people who will have the opportunity to vote for him or her at the next election. The type of work and the research involved will run the gamut of the interests of the people who live in your member's district or state. In your assignments, you can expect to look into why a constituent did not receive a Social Security check or provide information about services and benefits available to veterans in your member's state or district. Interns working with members from the western United States might be asked to look into issues surrounding the distribution of water resources among those states. Members from rural areas might ask their interns to look into agricultural programs or issues of rural economic development. Because personalized, attentive service to constituents is highly valued in a congressional office, you should not be surprised if you are assigned to coordinate tours of the Capitol and make other arrangements for constituents who visit Washington, D.C. On Capitol Hill, representational work is seen as intimately tied to your member's political well-being. Timely, accurate research that solves a constituent's problem serves both the constituent and the legislator.

In many cases, oversight research can be seen as another facet of constituent work. Several agencies of the national government regulate issues such as distribution of water resources, agricultural programs, and economic development. As questions and complaints about these programs come into the office, they may indicate areas in which these agencies and programs may be made more effective or responsive.

When you are conducting representational and oversight research, you will use a range of resources that explain the law and the activities of the executive branch agencies that carry out the laws.

U.S. Code

When Congress passes a public law, the various new requirements of the legislation are incorporated into the *U.S. Code*. Organized by title, or main subject, all of the laws regarding a given policy or program can be found in one place. Because of its dynamic nature, paper versions of the code are often out of date. A current electronic version of the *U.S. Code* can be accessed and searched through the Legislative Information System.

Federal Register and Code of Federal Regulations

Once Congress passes a bill and it is enacted into law, the executive branch agency responsible for implementing the law will usually write a series of rules governing the law's implementation. This process, called rulemaking, is documented in the *Federal Register.* Issued daily and running to sixty thousand pages a year, the *Federal Register* catalogs all the official activity of the Executive Office of the President as well as the departments, executive agencies, independent agencies, boards, commissions, and committees. Once an agency adopts a rule, it is codified in the *Code of Federal Regulations* (*CFR*). The *CFR* is the permanent listing of the rules by which laws are implemented and is organized according to the same system used in the *U.S. Code*. In your internship you might be asked to retrieve existing or proposed rules from either of these sources, as well as the public comments regarding those rules, which are also printed in the *Federal Register.* The *Federal Register* and the *Code of Federal Regulations* are published by the Government Printing Office and are available online at http://www.gpo.gov.

Executive Branch Resources

As the first branch of government, Congress writes the laws that create and fund executive branch agencies. As a congressional intern, you will be well placed to take advantage of the opportunities that come with agency efforts to maintain a positive working relationship with the national legislature. Every department and office of the executive branch has a congressional relations office staffed with officials who can provide data, copies of government documents, periodicals, and reference sources that explain the policies and programs for which they are responsible. Some offices, including the Executive Office of the President and military branches, maintain liaison offices on Capitol Hill to assist member offices with their concerns. A directory of liaison offices is available in each member office.

Legislative Branch Research Support

In addition to the research materials at your disposal from congressional sources, executive branch agencies, and private interest groups, there are several specialized agencies in the legislative branch that can assist you in your research efforts. These agencies include the Library of Congress (LOC), Congressional Research Service (CRS), Congressional Budget Office (CBO), and General Accounting Office (GAO).

The Library of Congress

The primary mission of the Library of Congress is to make a wide variety of materials representing the broad scope of human knowledge available to the U.S. Congress. The Library identifies, analyzes, and synthesizes this information to make it useful to the lawmakers who are the elected representatives of the American people. In addition to reference assistance, congressional offices may borrow books from the Library's extensive collections.

Congressional Research Service

Within the Library of Congress is the Congressional Research Service. CRS works exclusively as a nonpartisan analytical, research, and reference arm for Congress. CRS serves Congress throughout the legislative process by providing comprehensive legislative research, analysis, and information services that are timely, objective, nonpartisan, and confidential, thereby contributing to an informed national legislature. CRS staff provide analysis and information to members and congressional staff on the range of topics that are important to Congress. Services include online access to CRS products and services, plus links to public policy and legislative resources through the CRS website. In addition, CRS provides information, research, and bibliographic services by telephone or in person at research centers across Capitol Hill. CRS also offers an orientation program to congressional interns; upon completion of the orientation, interns are encouraged to use CRS centers for their research.

The Congressional Budget Office

The mission of the Congressional Budget Office is to provide Congress with objective, timely, nonpartisan analyses needed to make economic and budget decisions, and information and estimates required for the Congressional budget process. CBO prepares independent analyses and estimates relating to the budget and the economy and presents options and alternatives for Congress to consider. CBO prepares various types of analyses for Congress, including cost estimates for bills that individual members have introduced or plan to introduce. This subject matter gives CBO a broad reach, reflecting the wide array of activities that the federal budget covers and the major role the budget plays in the U.S. economy.

The General Accounting Office

The General Accounting Office is Congress's investigative arm. GAO exists to support Congress in meeting its constitutional responsibilities and to help improve the federal government's performance and accountability. GAO examines the use of public funds, evaluates federal programs and activities, and provides analyses, options, recommendations, and other assistance to help Congress make effective oversight, policy, and funding decisions. At the request of members and committees of Congress, GAO carries out a range of activities, including financial audits, program reviews and evaluations, analyses, investigations, and other services. GAO's activities are designed to ensure the executive branch's accountability to Congress under the Constitution and the government's accountability to the American people.

Conclusion: Don't Forget the Politics

The resources listed here are in no way complete; however, they will get you started in any of the areas of research you are likely to undertake as a congressional intern. As you consult the materials you gather from these sources, it is imperative that you follow the guidelines to answer the questions asked of you and to provide as complete an answer as you can given the available time and resources.

Equally important as you complete assignments is to be aware of the intensely political nature of the environment in which you are working. Keep in mind that each of the sources of information you utilize represents a set of political interests and expectations. Although the laws and rules governing their implementation may appear reasonably clear, information provided by public agencies in the executive branch and private interest groups quite reasonably will highlight their preferred policy positions. Remember that one political actor's preferred position seldom represents the entire story of a particular policy or program. As political actors pursuing their own interests, interest groups and executive branch agencies will sometimes select only the facts that best support their preferences. This seems obvious when we consider, for example, physicians who want public policies that help reduce tobacco-related deaths versus cigarette companies that want to be able to sell their product.

Keep in mind that these same rules apply to the various executive branch agencies. Officials from the Department of Health and Human Services responsible for smoking cessation efforts are likely to see the world differently from Department of Agriculture officials responsible for managing programs to assist tobacco farmers. The offices and departments within the executive branch encompass a wide range of origins, clienteles, and cultures. All of these factors may be reflected in the types of reports and information available from these executive branch offices.

In conclusion, research materials from any source may not present a balanced or complete picture of a particular policy question. In some instances, what is presented as a fact may be an assertion, a matter of preference, or an error. Working in such a politically charged environment places a special responsibility on you to keep a clear sense of the differences between facts, preferences, and speculation. In the end it is your responsibility to present information as completely and clearly as you are able. Successful research will often rely on the breadth of your sources and your ability to responsibly discern among a range of policy positions.

10

Presidential and Executive Branch Research

L. Elaine Halchin
CONGRESSIONAL RESEARCH SERVICE

You've done it. You've landed the internship you wanted and it's your first—or maybe your second or third—day on the job. Everything is going great until your boss asks you to find . . . an executive order issued by President John F. Kennedy, the section of the *CFR* that deals with federal building security, and a copy of OMB Circular A–76. What's an executive order? Is "*CFR*" some kind of code? And OMB Circular A–76 sounds like an official document, but where do you find it?

Not to worry. By the time you finish reading this chapter, you'll have a good idea of what your boss is talking about. And with a little practice and a few visits to the library to review the sources, documents, and publications discussed here, you will have mastered the primary sources for researching the executive branch.

This chapter begins with a brief description of how the executive branch is organized. An understanding of the different types of departments and agencies and where they are situated within the executive branch will help you to know where to look for materials. The second section covers primary sources of information about the executive branch and its activities. Government sources are essential, and for some research tasks, they are the only sources you can use. You will also find that nongovernment sources, which are examined in the third section, can be used to supplement government sources. They

139

may provide information not found in government documents, alert you to new developments, or offer a different perspective.

Executive Branch Organization

The Executive Office of the President, the fourteen executive departments, and numerous independent agencies, government corporations, boards, commissions, committees, and quasi-official agencies make up the executive branch. An invaluable reference for information about the executive branch (and the legislative and judicial branches too) is the *United States Government Manual.* Published annually by the National Archives and Records Administration (NARA) and printed by the Government Printing Office (GPO), the *Government Manual* contains comprehensive information about all executive branch organizations. The current edition (as well as several past editions) can be found online at http://www.access.gpo.gov/nara/nara001.html. The online editions allow you to search or browse for information, which is particularly useful if you are looking for a specific office or function but aren't sure where in the federal bureaucracy it's located.

Executive Office of the President

The Executive Office of the President (EOP) consists of organizations that immediately serve the president and includes his closest advisors. The EOP's composition may vary from president to president as components are added or abolished. If you're asked to find information about an EOP component or organization, your first step may be to check the current *Government Manual* to determine whether the organization still exists.

The following EOP organizations have existed for some time:

White House Office
Office of the Vice President
Council of Economic Advisers
Council on Environmental Quality
National Security Council (NSC)

Office of Administration
Office of Management and Budget (OMB)
Office of National Drug Control Policy
Office of Policy Development
Domestic Policy Council
National Economic Council
Office of Science and Technology Policy
Office of the United States Trade Representative.

One newly created office in the EOP is the Office of Homeland Security, which was created by President George W. Bush following the September 11 terrorist attacks.

The Executive Departments

The fourteen executive departments are as follows: Agriculture, Commerce, Defense, Education, Energy, Health and Human Services, Housing and Urban Development, Interior, Justice, Labor, State, Transportation, Treasury, and Veterans Affairs. A secretary heads each executive department except for the Department of Justice, which is headed by the attorney general.

Within the executive departments, you'll find a variety of subordinate organizations. Because it's possible to confuse subordinate organizations with independent agencies, you may want to scan the *Government Manual* to get an idea of which organizations belong to executive departments. The following are well-known subordinate organizations (and their parent departments): the Federal Bureau of Investigation (FBI) and the Drug Enforcement Administration (DEA) (Department of Justice); the Food and Drug Administration (FDA) and the National Institutes of Health (Department of Health and Human Services); the National Park Service and the Bureau of Indian Affairs (Department of the Interior); and the Federal Aviation Administration and the Federal Highway Administration (Department of Transportation). The Air Force, Army, and Navy Departments warrant special mention because, although they are called "departments," they are located within the Department of Defense.

Independent Agencies

Nearly sixty independent agencies and government corporations are found in the executive branch, as are numerous boards, commissions, committees, and quasi-official agencies. Some of the better known independent agencies, government corporations, and quasi-official agencies are the Central Intelligence Agency (CIA), the Environmental Protection Agency (EPA), the Federal Deposit Insurance Corporation (FDIC), the Federal Emergency Management Agency (FEMA), the General Services Administration (GSA), the National Aeronautics and Space Administration (NASA), the National Archives and Records Administration (NARA), the Office of Personnel Management (OPM), the Peace Corps, the Smithsonian Institution, and the U.S. Postal Service (USPS). A complete list of these organizations, and comprehensive information about each, may be found in the *Government Manual.* Boards, commissions, and committees, such as the Appalachian Regional Commission and the National Park Foundation, also are listed in the *Government Manual.* Many executive branch organizations maintain websites. If you don't know what the Web address is, you should be able to find a link at First-Gov, http://firstgov.gov, the official U.S. government portal.

Government Sources of Information

Executive Branch Sources

Whether you're looking for a regulation, an executive order, a meeting notice, or a president's speech, you'll find it in one (or more) of the National Archives and Records Administration's publications. NARA is an independent federal agency. In addition to preserving the cornerstone documents of our government, including the Declaration of Independence and the Constitution of the United States, NARA documents the federal government's activities through the publication of "laws, regulations, and Presidential and other public documents." Visit the *Federal Register Publications System* website, at http://www.nara.gov/fedreg/nf-pubs.html, for more information about and links to the publications discussed here.

Federal Register

One of the most useful NARA publications is the *Federal Register*, which is available in print, online at http://www.merrimack.nara.gov, and on microfiche. Published each federal workday, it documents the activities of the executive branch. The contents of the print version are organized into four categories: presidential documents (for example, executive orders and proclamations), rules and regulations (including policy statements and interpretations of rules), proposed rules, and notices (scheduled hearings and meetings open to the public, grant applications, administrative orders, and the like). (See Box 10.1.) The daily table of contents in both the print and electronic versions is organized alphabetically by agency and department, and each document is a separate entry. The online table of contents includes hyperlinks to entries in that day's issue of the *Federal Register*. The only time you'll need to remember that the *Federal Register* is organized by category is when you're browsing through an issue or issues and need to know in which section or category to look. Otherwise, you'll use a hyperlink (online) or page number (print) to take you to the desired entry.

Annual indexes and the current cumulative index will help you find documents published in the *Federal Register*. An annual index includes every document published during a calendar year. The current cumulative index contains every document published during the current

---

Box 10.1 Rules and regulations.

Federal agencies issue regulations, also known as "rules." Developing a regulation usually involves a process known as the notice and comment procedure. An agency publishes a public notice of a proposed rule in the *Federal Register*. An individual or organization may comment on the proposed rule. In addition to publishing the final rule or regulation, an agency must include any significant issues that were raised by the comments and explain how the agency responded to those comments, including any changes made to the rule. So the *Federal Register* is useful not only for tracking proposed and final rules but also for learning why an agency developed a rule in a particular way.

year through the end of the previous month. While both types of indexes are available online (as well as in print), they do not include links to documents. However, once you have found a document in one of the indexes, you'll be able to use its page number to find it in the GPO Access *Federal Register*, which is available at http://www.access.gpo.gov/su_docs/aces/aces140.html. Index entries begin with the agency that issued the document and then list the topics.

Regularly scanning the table of contents of current issues of the *Federal Register* will help you track executive branch activities. For example, you may want to review the subjects of recent executive orders or find out whether a proposed rule has been finalized. The online version of the *Federal Register*, at http://www.merrimack.nara.gov, is well suited for this task.

When you cite information taken from the *Federal Register*, you'll need to include all the facts of publication, just as you do when citing a book or a journal article. The citation should appear in the following format:

[name of department, agency, or office], "[title of entry]," *Federal Register*, vol. [volume number], no. [issue number], [date], p. [page number].

In 2001, the Fish and Wildlife Service posted a notice of a permit application:

Department of the Interior, Fish and Wildlife Service, "Endangered and Threatened Species Permit Application," *Federal Register*, vol. 66, no. 87, May 4, 2001, p. 22593.

Because the Fish and Wildlife Service is a subunit of the Department of the Interior, both organizations are listed in the *Federal Register*. If the Department of the Interior had issued this notice, it would be the only organization listed.

A good rule of thumb for any source is to provide complete information in your citations so that you or someone who is reading your work will be able to find the original source.

Code of Federal Regulations

The *Code of Federal Regulations* (CFR) is another very useful document published by NARA. Unlike the *Federal Register*, which publishes proposed and final regulations on a daily basis and by agency, the *CFR* is published annually and is a codification of general and permanent (that is, final) regulations that have been published in the *Federal Register*. The *CFR* groups regulations by general subject areas, which are called "titles." There are fifty titles in the *CFR*. Each title consists of chapters, which are broken down into parts, subparts, and sections, the smallest element. The accepted form of citation is "[title number] CFR [section number]." For example, Title 24 contains regulations pertaining to the Department of Housing and Urban Development, and 24 CFR 583.110 is the section on grants for new construction (under Housing and Urban Development's Supportive Housing Program). Armed with title and section numbers, you'll be able to find this regulation. (See Box 10.2.)

Box 10.2 *USC* and *CFR* titles.

Both the *U.S. Code* and the *Code of Federal Regulations* are organized by titles. However, subject areas do not necessarily have the same title number in both the *USC* and the *CFR*. This means that you cannot expect to find regulations and statutes pertaining to the same subject are under the same title number in both the *USC* and the *CFR*. These are some of the titles that have different subject areas in the *USC* and the *CFR*.

Title	U.S. Code	Code of Federal Regulations
Title 4	Flag and Seal, Seat of Govt. and the States	Accounts
Title 14	Coast Guard	Aeronautics and Space
Title 20	Education	Employees' Benefits
Title 35	Patents	Panama Canal
Title 50	War and National Defense	Wildlife and Fisheries

The *CFR* is updated annually on a quarterly basis, which means that selected titles are updated each quarter and the entire set of *CFR* volumes is updated annually. Because changes affecting the *CFR* occur daily, the Government Printing Office (GPO) publishes and makes available online a publication that lists *CFR* sections affected by changes published in the *Federal Register.* This publication is titled the *Federal Register: The LSA* (for *List of Sections Affected*). It is possible to check for changes to the *CFR* by browsing or searching the *LSA* online. This service is available at http://www.access.gpo.gov/nara.lsa and includes information on how to search the *LSA*. The list of *CFR* sections affected by entries in the daily *Federal Register* is available online at http://www.access.gpo.gov/nara/lsa/curlist.html.

Codification, whereby regulations are grouped by topic, is what makes the *CFR* a particularly useful tool. If you've been asked to find the set of regulations that pertains to a specific topic, you'll begin with the "table of titles." Located in the annual index (print version) and available online at http://www.access.gpo.gov/nara/cfr/cfr-table-search.html, the table lists all fifty titles. Using this table, you would identify the appropriate title. By clicking on that title, you reach a list of chapters; by clicking on a chapter, you reach a list of parts; and so on. Although it is more convenient to browse online, the print version of the *CFR* also includes lists of chapters, parts, subparts, and sections that make up a title.

The *Code of Federal Regulations* can be confusing. Certain parts of the *CFR* have the same acronym; others have similar-sounding names. The *CFR* includes Federal Travel Regulations (FTR), Title 41 CFR chapters 300–304; the Federal Acquisition Regulations (FAR), Title 48 CFR; and the Federal Aviation Regulations (FAR), Title 14 CFR. As always, get as much information as you can on your research project and ask a lot of questions. A good understanding of your research assignment can save everyone a lot of time and prevent a great deal of confusion.

Weekly Compilation of Presidential Documents

The *Weekly Compilation of Presidential Documents*, popularly known as the *Weekly Comp*, is published every Monday and contains the full text of presidential statements, addresses, messages, remarks, and any other materials released by the White House press secretary. It also includes items published in the *Federal Register*, as well as bill signings, communications to Congress, communications to federal agencies, interviews with the news media, nominations submitted to the Senate, letters and messages, meetings with foreign leaders, military orders, joint statements, and other notices. In short, the *Weekly Comp* is a comprehensive source of information about a president's activities and actions.

Unless you already know the specific document and the date it was released, you will want to use a quarterly, semiannual, or annual index. Each one indexes presidential materials by subject, name, and document category. For example, using the *Weekly Comp*, you'll be able to locate all of President Jimmy Carter's statements on the Iran hostage crisis, as well as other related materials. You could also find out how many bills President George W. Bush signed during his first year in office or see the complete text of President Bill Clinton's interview with Dan Rather in 1999.

As with other NARA publications, the *Weekly Compilation of Presidential Documents* is available in print and electronically, at http://www.access.gpo.gov/nara/nara003.html. When citing the *Weekly Comp*, use this format:

U.S. President ([president's last name]), "[title of entry]," *Weekly Compilation of Presidential Documents*, vol. [number], [date of issue], p. [number].

For example:

U.S. President (Clinton), "Remarks on Signing a Proclamation Establishing the Giant Sequoia National Monument in Sequoia National Forest, California," *Weekly Compilation of Presidential Documents*, vol. 36, April 24, 2000, p. 843.

Public Papers of the Presidents

Published beginning in 1957, the *Public Papers of the Presidents* currently contains the presidents' public writings, addresses, and remarks from the Hoover, Truman, Eisenhower, Kennedy, Johnson, Nixon, Ford, Carter, Reagan, Bush, and Clinton administrations. The material is presented in chronological order, and the date shown is the date of the event or statement unless otherwise noted. Volumes are published approximately twice a year. The index for each volume contains name and subject indexes and a list of documents. The appendixes include a list of the president's daily schedule and meetings; nominations submitted to the Senate; and a table of executive orders, proclamations, and other materials published in the *Federal Register*. Also in the appendixes is a list of materials released by the White House press secretary, but the full text of these is not printed in the *Public Papers*.

Printed volumes are available for the presidencies of Herbert Hoover, Harry S Truman, Dwight D. Eisenhower, John F. Kennedy, Lyndon B. Johnson, Richard M. Nixon, Jimmy Carter, Ronald Reagan, George H. W. Bush, and William J. Clinton. Some of President Clinton's volumes are available electronically, and NARA continues to add other volumes from his presidency. The public papers of President Bush and President Reagan are available online at their respective presidential libraries.

For citing material found in the *Public Papers*, use the same format as you would use for citing the *Weekly Compilation of Presidential Documents*.

Executive Orders

Though not provided for in the Constitution, executive orders are a primary means for a president to act unilaterally, since they do not require the approval of Congress. Presidents use executive orders to recognize groups and organizations, establish commissions and committees, establish policy and alter administrative and regulatory policy, and make symbolic statements. Executive orders can be found in the *Federal Register* as well as the *Weekly Compilation of Presidential Documents*.

The proper way to cite an executive order is:

U.S. President ([president's last name]), "[title of the executive order]," Executive Order [number], *Federal Register,* vol. [number], [date], p. [number].

Executive Order 11398 would be cited as follows:

U.S. President (Johnson), "Establishing the President's Council on Physical Fitness and Sports," Executive Order 11398, *Federal Register,* vol. 33, March 6, 1968, p. 4169.

The National Archives and Records Administration provides another useful tool on its website: the Executive Orders Disposition Table. The table lists by year the executive orders issued by the presidents, beginning with Franklin D. Roosevelt. One advantage of this tool is that, beginning with President Clinton, each table includes links to the full text of executive orders. Even though links to the texts of previous executive orders are not available, each disposition table provides *Federal Register* citations, which you can use to find orders in the print version. Another useful feature of each table is that it shows each executive order's current status. Executive orders may be amended, revoked, modified, or superseded by a subsequent executive order (or orders). The disposition tables note whether an order has been changed and, if so, include the number of the subsequent executive order that effected the change. (See Box 10.3.)

Box 10.3 Government resources at a glance.

What you want . . .	*Where to find it . . .*
Recent executive order	Disposition Table of Executive Orders
Recently- issued regulations	*Federal Register*
Regulations on a specific topic	*Code of Federal Regulations*
Department/agency information	*Government Manual* or FirstGov website
Presidential documents	*Weekly Compilation of Presidential Documents* or *Public Papers of the Presidents*

Information from Departments and Agencies

As a result of the Internet, it is now easier than ever to obtain information from and about an executive branch department or agency and its activities, publications, and documents. The First-Gov website, at http://firstgov.gov, provides links to federal agencies and departments, the legislative and judicial branches, and a number of subject areas. Website content varies from agency to agency, but generally you can find the agency's mission statement; press releases, statements, and announcements; and information about its programs, policies, and activities. When the information you're seeking is not on the website and is not available from other sources, you may need to contact someone directly at the agency or department. Federal government websites also usually provide telephone numbers for their public relations offices or a "contact us" link. (Department and agency descriptions in the *Government Manual* usually include contact information for their congressional liaisons.)

GSA, OMB, and OPM

Three executive branch organizations that you'll want to familiarize yourself with are the General Services Administration (GSA), Office of Management and Budget (OMB), and Office of Personnel Management (OPM). Unlike most agencies and departments, which have specific policy subject areas, the policies, programs, and activities of GSA, OMB, and OPM pertain to the operation of the executive branch.

- The General Services Administration establishes policy and maintains programs related to the management of government property and records; the procurement and distribution of supplies; the management of real and personal property; information technology; and transportation, traffic, and communications management. For more information about GSA, visit its website, at http://www.gsa.gov.
- The Office of Management and Budget assists the president in the preparation and administration of the federal budget and

develops organization and management procedures for the executive branch. Because it is part of the Executive Office of the President, the OMB website can be accessed through the White House website, http://www.whitehouse.gov/omb.

- The Office of Personnel Management develops policies and programs relating to the recruitment, management, promotion, and retention of federal government employees. OPM helps agencies and departments fulfill their human resource responsibilities. You'll find OPM's website at http://www.opm.gov.

The General Accounting Office

The General Accounting Office (GAO), the investigative arm of Congress, is an excellent source of information about government agencies and departments, programs, and operations. Its website is found at http://www.gao.gov. GAO's published reports and testimony, which also are available online, offer a wealth of information about executive branch activities and topics, ranging from veterans' health care issues and management challenges facing the National Aeronautics and Space Administration to securities regulations and implementation of the Federal Activities Inventory Reform (FAIR) Act.

GAO publishes a monthly catalogue that lists the reports released each month. A more timely and convenient way of keeping track of recent reports is to subscribe to GAO's daily email alert. The GAO website includes a feature, "Find GAO Reports," that enables you to search abstracts of all reports and testimony from January 1, 1975, to the present. Links are provided to reports and testimony that are available electronically. You may download reports from the GAO website or order them by telephone, mail, or fax (ordering information is found on the website). If you're seeking a report that was issued within the past month, you can use the "Reports and Testimony" database to locate the item. The proper format for citing GAO reports is as follows:

U.S. General Accounting Office, [title of report in italics], GAO report [number of report] (Washington: [date of report]), p. [page number].

The citation for a GAO report issued in 1999 on the Olympic Games would read like this:

U.S. General Accounting Office, *Olympic Games: Preliminary Information on Federal Funding and Support*, GAO report GGD–00–44 (Washington: Dec. 21, 1999), p. 3.

Other Government Sources

If your internship is in Washington, D.C., you'll discover other legislative sources of information, such as congressional committee hearings, useful to your study of the executive branch. A hearing that examines department or agency activities or includes officials from the executive branch on the panel of witnesses may yield information not available elsewhere. Comprehensive daily committee schedules for the Senate and the House of Representatives may be accessed by using Thomas, a legislative information website administered by the Library of Congress, found at http://www.thomas.loc.gov. Committee schedules also are published in the two major Washington, D.C., newspapers, the *Washington Post* and *Washington Times*.

If a hearing relevant to your research is scheduled, you may want to attend or at least obtain copies of witnesses' prepared statements. Usually, copies are available at a hearing and also may be made available through the appropriate committee's or subcommittee's website. Hearing transcripts are potentially even more useful because, in addition to witnesses' prepared statements, they include transcripts of any discussion or question-and-answer sessions that took place during the hearing. Generally, however, it takes several months to produce and publish hearing transcripts, which is why you'll want to obtain copies of witnesses' statements for a current hearing. Transcripts from past hearings may be found in a research library or at committee or subcommittee websites.

If you're working for a member of Congress or a congressional committee, you'll be able to access the Legislative Information System (LIS), which is administered by the Congressional Research Service (a component of the Library of Congress). Although this website focuses on the legislative branch, it includes some information pertaining to the executive branch, such as the status of presidential nominations. Only those nominations that require Senate approval are listed on LIS. LIS also includes committee schedule information for the Senate and the House of Representatives.

Nongovernment Sources of Information

Nongovernment sources of information can also provide information, data, and analyses not found—or not readily available from—government sources. For example, you might find an academic paper on regulations from George Mason University's Mercatus Center that includes data and analysis on the pace of rulemaking at various times in a president's term.

Nongovernmental sources are useful because they can provide varying perspectives on an issue. Examining information from a variety of sources could help you uncover a fresh perspective or an argument that has not been widely reported. Remember, though, that you must assess the veracity, accuracy, and credibility of new, untested sources and discern the author's objectives.

Publications That Focus on Government

As you become more familiar with your responsibilities, your work, and the resources available to you, you'll discover there are a number of publications that focus exclusively on the federal government. *Government Executive* magazine, the *Federal Times*, and the *Federal Employees News Digest* are three of the better-known publications that report exclusively on the federal government and that are available without a subscription. *Government Executive*, available at http://www.govexec.com, and the *Federal Times*, at http://www.federaltimes.com, regularly report on management issues, government employee travel, and pay and benefits. The *Federal Employees News*

Digest, at http://www.fendonline.com, is another excellent source for the latest information on civil service issues. All three are available both online and in print and offer daily email alerts.

The format for citing a magazine or journal article is:

[author's name], "[title of article]," [title of journal or article, in italics], vol. [volume number], [date of issue], p. [page number].

An article from *Government Executive* would be cited as follows:

Katherine McIntire Peters, "Pulling Together," *Government Executive,* vol. 33, October 2001, p. 8.

Think Tanks

Think tanks offer reports, studies, statements, opinion pieces, press conferences, and seminars, all of which are potentially useful sources of information for you. Some of the better-known think tanks based in Washington, D.C., are the American Enterprise Institute, Brookings Institution, Cato Institute, Heritage Foundation, and Mercatus Center at George Mason University. The easiest way to find these organizations and what they have to offer is to visit their websites.

Print Media

Reading a reputable local newspaper and a weekly newsmagazine, such as the *Economist, Newsweek, Time,* or *U.S. News and World Report,* is essential for following executive branch activities and for learning about related events and news. If you're interning in Washington, D.C., you'll want to read the *Washington Post* or the *Washington Times.* The citation format for a newspaper is similar to that for a magazine or journal article. However, there are two differences. For a newspaper citation, include the complete date (month, day, and year) and the newspaper section (such as A, B, C) as well as the page number. It is permissible to combine the newspaper section and page number, as in p. A7.

Knowing Your Sources

The nongovernment sources mentioned here are some of the better known and more reliable sources. This does not mean, though, that other sources you discover are not as valuable or useful. However, you need to be aware that not all sources are equally credible or accurate, which is particularly true for Internet sites. Also, many sources are associated with a particular ideology. There is nothing wrong with using such sources, as long as the information is accurate and credible. The key is to examine critically any new source you plan to use in your work.

Conclusion

Now that you know how to find regulations, executive orders, and information about executive departments, don't forget that doing research is a creative process. Because this chapter, as a foundation for executive branch research, covers long-established government sources and essential types of information, it portrays research as a "follow-the-recipe" process. In some cases, research is simply a matter of following known and specific steps. But sometimes you'll have to rely on your ingenuity and problem-solving skills to find the information you need. Mastering the sources presented here is only the first step. You'll also want to explore new sources and develop research strategies tailored to your work.

11

Judicial and Legal Research

Ryan Petersen
COLLEGE OF THE REDWOODS

To an undergraduate with no formal training in the law, conducting legal research can seem a daunting task. How do I go about locating the Gun-Free School Zones Act of 1990? What is *18 U.S.C. 922 (q)(1)(A)* and where can I find it? Where do I find the Supreme Court's opinion in *United States v. Lopez*? What does *514 U.S. 549* refer to? These are the types of questions you may find yourself asking during your political internship. Though most specialized legal work will be left to staffers with law degrees, interns will often be asked to conduct at least some basic legal research. This chapter is designed to familiarize you with the process of researching and citing the law.

What Is the Law?

As you probably recall from your political science classes (or at least from those old *Schoolhouse Rock* cartoons), the legislative branch is primarily responsible for "making" the law. Indeed, "statutes" (bills passed by both houses of Congress and then signed into law by the president) comprise one of the primary categories of what we call "the law."

But what happens when the U.S. Supreme Court declares a statute unconstitutional? What about regulations handed down by an executive agency like the Federal Aviation Administration? In our complex system of government, "the law" isn't just those bills passed by Congress and signed by the president. The law also includes administrative regulations and judicial interpretation. And this is just at the national level! Each state has its own set of statutes, administrative regulations, and court decisions. Though we will discuss all of these sources of law to some degree, the emphasis of this chapter will be on finding and citing federal statutes as organized in the *Statutes at Large* and the *United States Code* and locating Supreme Court decisions compiled in *United States Reports*.

Where Can I Conduct Legal Research?

Not so long ago, conducting legal research required a trip to a major academic, government, or law library. Indeed, if you plan to engage in serious legal research, a good old-fashioned law library is still your best bet. Furthermore, all of the sources of law that we will discuss (*Statutes at Large, U.S. Code, U.S. Reports*, etc.) can still be found in bound volumes and are available in most major libraries. As a practical matter, however, most legal research can now be conducted via the Internet (see Box 11.1: Legal Research on the Internet).

Although the Internet has made legal research much easier and significantly faster, be forewarned that website addresses change, webpages come and go with great frequency, and many of the best sites for legal research are available only with a paid subscription. Even if you intend to do all of your research online, it's important to be familiar with the various bound volumes, as their organization still dictates proper citation format and also determines how you will be able to conduct many of your online searches.

Researching Statutes

When one thinks of "the law," one most likely thinks of statutes—all of the bills passed by Congress and signed into law by the president. There are two primary sources for researching federal statutes, the *Statutes at Large* and the *U.S. Code*. Each source has different content and a different organization.

Box 11.1 Legal Research on the Internet.

The Internet has greatly simplified basic legal research. No longer do you have to make a special trip to a law library if you simply want to find a statute or court decision. There are a number of excellent subscription services (most notably Lexis-Nexis and Westlaw) that you may be able to access through a law school, university, or government library (make sure to ask a librarian for assistance). If you don't have access to a pay site, there are also a number of free websites offering much of the same information.

Free Websites for Conducting Legal Research:

FindLaw—http://www.findlaw.com
An excellent website containing a wealth of information, including *U.S. Code*, federal regulations, case law, and links to state resources. Searchable by several methods, such as citation, title, and keyword.

Legal Information Institute (Cornell Law School)—
http://www.law.cornell.edu
Another outstanding website with a tremendous amount of information, including *U.S. Code*, federal regulations, case law, and links to state information. Searchable by a variety of methods, such as case name listings, subject listings, citations, and keyword.

U.S. House of Representatives—http://www.house.gov/uscode
Part of the House of Representatives official website. Provides database of *U.S. Code* searchable by title and section or keyword.

Statutes at Large

The *Statutes at Large* contains the full text of all the laws passed since the first session of Congress, organized in chronological order. Each volume contains the legislation passed by a particular session of Congress, and the citation format is based on the volume and page number (see Box 11.2: Understanding Legal Citation: *Statutes at Large*). The *Statutes at Large* can help you identify the various provisions of a particular law, but beyond that, it can be a

Box 11.2 Understanding legal citation: *Statutes at Large.*

The *Statutes at Large* are organized chronologically, so the citation format is simply based on volume and page number. The citation contains the volume number (e.g. 104), followed by the abbreviation for the source (e.g. Stat. for *Statutes at Large*) followed by the page number where the statute begins (e.g. 4844). Below is the citation for the Gun-Free School Zones Act of 1990.

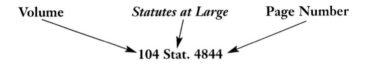

Thus, if you wanted to find the text of the *Gun-Free School Zones Act of 1990*, you would go to volume 104 of the *Statutes at Large* and turn to page 4844.

cumbersome tool. If you don't have a citation or don't know the date of the law's passage, the *Statutes at Large* is of limited value. If you know the approximate time period that a bill was signed into law, you can usually track down the specific date in outside sources like the *Congressional Quarterly Annual Report*.

The U.S. Code

Somewhat more useful to the researcher is the *U.S. Code* (or *USC*), which organizes federal statutes by subject into fifty separate titles (see Box 11.3: Titles of the *U.S. Code*). Like the *Statutes at Large*, the *USC* is available in bound volumes in most major libraries, but unlike the *Statutes*, it is also readily available on a number of free websites.

Searching the *USC* is quite easy and can be done by using the subject headings of the titles, sections, and subsections or by using volume and page numbers, provided you already have a citation for the part of the *Code* you need to find. Additionally, most online

Box 11.3 Titles of the *U.S. Code.*

Title 1   General Provisions
Title 2   The Congress
Title 3   The President
Title 4   Flag and Seal, Seat of Government, and the States
Title 5   Government Organization and Employees
Title 6   Surety Bonds (Repealed)
Title 7   Agriculture
Title 8   Aliens and Nationality
Title 9   Arbitration
Title 10 Armed Forces
Title 11 Bankruptcy
Title 12 Banks and Banking
Title 13 Census
Title 14 Coast Guard
Title 15 Commerce and Trade
Title 16 Conservation
Title 17 Copyrights
Title 18 Crimes and Criminal Procedure
Title 19 Customs Duties
Title 20 Education
Title 21 Food and Drugs
Title 22 Foreign Relations and Intercourse
Title 23 Highways
Title 24 Hospitals and Asylums
Title 25 Indians
Title 26 Internal Revenue Code
Title 27 Intoxicating Liquors

Title 28 Judiciary and Judicial Procedure
Title 29 Labor
Title 30 Mineral Lands and Mining
Title 31 Money and Finance
Title 32 National Guard
Title 33 Navigation and Navigable Waters
Title 34 Navy (Repealed)
Title 35 Patents
Title 36 Patriotic Societies and Observances
Title 37 Pay and Allowances of the Uniformed Services
Title 38 Veterans' Benefits
Title 39 Postal Service
Title 40 Public Buildings, Property, and Works
Title 41 Public Contracts
Title 42 The Public Health and Welfare
Title 43 Public Lands
Title 44 Public Printing and Documents
Title 45 Railroads
Title 46 Shipping
Title 47 Telegraphs, Telephones, and Radiotelegraphs
Title 48 Territories and Insular Possessions
Title 49 Transportation
Title 50 War and National Defense

Box 11.4 Understanding legal citation: *U.S. Code.*

Once you are familiar with the organization of the *U.S. Code*, the citation format is fairly straightforward. The citation contains the title number (e.g. 18), followed by the abbreviation for the source (e.g. *U.S.C.* for *United States Code*) followed by the section number (e.g. 922), followed by any additional subsection or paragraph numbers (e.g. (q)(1)(A)). Below is the citation for the title and section of *U.S. Code* amended by the *Gun-Free School Zones Act of 1990*.

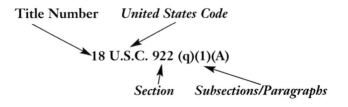

Occasionally, you may also see the section symbol (§) inserted between the "*U.S.C.*" and the section number. Also note that online databases will still organize *U.S. Code* by title and section, so searching and citation remains the same whether using bound volumes or a website.

databases will allow you to search the entire *USC* by keyword or phrase (see Box 11.4: Understanding Legal Citation: *U.S. Code*).

Researching Case Law

The term "case law" simply refers to the body of judicial decisions that are handed down by the courts when they interpret the law. As mentioned earlier, this is an important component of the broader conception of the law as it exists in the United States. When a court hands down a decision, the judge or judges ("justices" in the case of the U.S. Supreme Court) provide written explanations of their decision, which are called "opinions." When more than one judge or justice hears a case (such as with the U.S. Supreme Court), the legally binding decision reached by a majority of the court is known as the "opinion of the court." Justices who agreed with the outcome of the court's decision but had different reasons for reaching that decision write "concurring opinions." Finally, those justices who disagreed with the decision reached by the court write "dissenting opinions." For each case, all of these opinions along with a "syllabus" (a brief summary of the case) are compiled into bound volumes called "court reporters."

Supreme Court Reporters

There are three widely used court reporters that contain the opinions of the U.S. Supreme Court. *United States Reports* is the official reporter for the Supreme Court. Organized chronologically and indexed by subject, *U.S. Reports* is cited by volume and page number (see Box 11.5: Understanding Legal Citation: Case Law). Additionally, there are two privately published Supreme Court reporters, *United States Supreme Court Reports—Lawyers' Edition* and the *Supreme Court Reporter.* Both are organized and cited by volume and page number in a manner similar to *U.S. Reports* but contain additional annotations not found in the official reporter.

Other Court Reporters

Just as there are court reporters for the decisions of the U.S. Supreme Court, so too are there reporters for both the lower federal courts and state court systems. The opinions of United States Courts of Appeals can be found in the *Federal Reporter* (abbreviated F. 3d), and selected opinions from United States District Courts can be found in the *Federal Supplement* (abbreviated F. Supp.). Both are organized and cited in the same fashion as the Supreme Court reporters discussed above.

You may also find that you need to conduct research involving state court opinions. Most states publish reporters for their own court systems that are similar in function and organization to those found at the federal level. Additionally, some privately published "regional" reporters covering several states are available. If you

Box 11.5 Understanding legal citation: court reporters.

Whether you are trying to find a case using a citation or need to cite a case that you've found, the format utilized by all court reporters is essentially the same. The citation contains the name of the case in italics (e.g. *U.S. v. Lopez*), followed by the number of the bound volume in which the case is located (e.g. 514) followed by the abbreviation of the court reporter (e.g. U.S. for *United States Reports*), followed by the page number where the opinion begins (e.g. 549), followed by the year of the decision (e.g. 1995). Below is the citation from the official court reporter for the U.S. Supreme Court, *United States Reports,* for the case in which the Supreme Court struck down the *Gun-Free School Zones Act of 1990.*

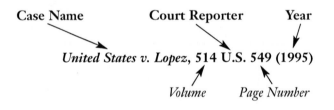

If you were citing the same case from one of the unofficial Supreme Court reporters, the citation would be *United States v. Lopez*, 131 L.Ed.2d 626 (1995) for *United States Supreme Court Reports—Lawyers' Edition* and *United States v. Lopez*, 115 Sup.Ct. 1624 (1995) for *Supreme Court Reporter.* Keep in mind that when conducting your research online, cases are still organized by volume and page number (generally the volume and page numbers from *U.S. Reports*). Thus, while you may be able to search online by subject or keyword, the fastest method of locating cases will still be to use a volume and page number citation. Furthermore, you will still cite cases by volume and page number when using an online database. It is also important to note that, prior to 1875, *U.S. Reports* was cited using the last name of the actual "Reporter of the Court" rather than the "U.S." abbreviation (the volume and page number format remains the same). So, for example, *Marbury v. Madison* would be cited as "1 Cranch 137" rather than "1 U.S. 137."

need to conduct only a little basic research—retrieving a case or finding a citation—you will probably be able to figure out enough about how your state's court reporters are organized to complete your assigned task. However, if you plan to conduct a significant amount of legal research at the state level, it would be a good idea to consult someone familiar with the court reporters in your particular state.

A Word on Citators

Most of the legal research you will do as an intern will simply involve using citations to retrieve particular statutes or cases. However, it is possible that you may be asked to conduct more intensive research into a particular statute, court decision, or general area of the law. Although finding and citing the law is relatively easy once you've learned something about the various sources available and how they're organized, making sure that the law you have found is still valid requires an additional, somewhat more difficult step.

The last thing you want to do is to report to your supervisor that something is "good law" when, in fact, it has been amended, repealed, or overturned by judicial action. Take our example of the Gun-Free School Zones Act of 1990. If you simply referred to the *Statutes at Large* or the *U.S. Code*, you wouldn't know that the act was struck down by the Supreme Court in *United States v. Lopez*. Even supposing you were familiar with the *Lopez* case and knew that the Supreme Court declared the Gun-Free School Zones Act unconstitutional, you still couldn't be assured that *Lopez* was valid, as it is quite possible the Court reversed itself in a subsequent case. This is where you will need to utilize what is known as a "citator," the best-known and readily available being *Shepard's Citations*.

Different *Shepard's* citators cover particular types of law (statutes, court decisions, etc.). You will be able to locate a particular statute or case in the appropriate citator by using the citation for the case or statute you are researching. *Shepard's* then lists the citations for each subsequent legislative action or court decision impacting the statute or case you are interested in. You will still need to locate and read the statutory changes and court decisions listed in *Shepard's* in order to determine precisely what has changed, which can be a time-consuming process to say the least.

As you have probably ascertained by now, "Shepardizing" is not an especially easy process for the beginner. Should you find that you need to Shepardize a particular statute or case, I highly recommended that you consult a comprehensive legal research manual (which should have a complete chapter on citators and Shepardizing) or, better yet, seek the assistance of a specialized law or reference librarian.

Other Legal Research

Federal Regulations

In addition to statute and case law, you may also need to conduct research on regulations issued by executive agencies. Federal regulations are published in two official sources. The *Federal Register* is similar in organization and function to the *Statutes at Large*, listing all federal regulations in chronological order. The *Code of Federal Regulations* (*CFR*) is the other source for obtaining information on regulations. Just as statutes are codified by topic in the *U.S. Code*, regulations are similarly organized in the *CFR*. For more information on finding and citing federal regulations, see Chapter 10 of this book, "Presidential and Executive Branch Research."

State Laws, Regulations, and Court Decisions

Depending on the nature of your internship, you may also find yourself having to conduct legal research at the state level. Although describing the sources and indexing methods for the laws, regulations, and court decisions of all fifty states is impossible in this chapter, most are compiled and organized in a similar fashion to their federal equivalents. Once you have learned the basics of legal research at the federal level, you should have little difficulty adapting to the particulars of your state's laws.

Legal Encyclopedias

References such as the *Oxford Companion to the Supreme Court of the United States* and *A Practical Companion to the U.S. Constitution* provide yet other sources of information for conducting basic legal research. Most of these volumes contain brief summaries of major Supreme Court decisions as well as entries for particular areas of the law ("interstate commerce," "freedom of speech," or "federalism," for example). Such encyclopedias are particularly useful as starting points before beginning more in-depth legal research or for reference when only a brief summary of the law is required.

Conclusion

As an intern, you may find the legal research you are assigned difficult at first. The long strings of numbers and abbreviations can be intimidating to someone without formal legal training. But once you know where to find the various sources of the law and understand how those sources are organized, the numbers and abbreviations will all begin to make sense, and basic legal research will become a relatively easy task.

For Further Reading

Legal Research Manuals

Cohen, Morris L., and Kent C. Olson. *Legal Research in a Nutshell.* 6th ed. St. Paul: West, 1996.

Elias, Stephen, Susan Levinkind, and Janet Portman. *Legal Research: How to Find and Understand the Law.* 7th ed. Berkeley: Nolo, 1999.

Melone, Albert P., and Carl Kalvelage. *Primer on Constitutional Law.* Pacific Palisades, Calif.: Palisades, 1982.

Legal Encyclopedias

Hall, Kermit (editor). *The Oxford Companion to the Supreme Court of the United States.* 1st ed. New York: Oxford University Press, 1992.

Lieberman, Jethro Koller. *A Practical Companion to the Constitution: How the Supreme Court Has Ruled on Issues from Abortion to Zoning.* 2nd ed. Berkeley and Los Angeles: University of California Press, 1999.

Witt, Elder. *Congressional Quarterly's Guide to the U.S. Supreme Court.* 2nd ed. Washington, D.C.: CQ Press, 1990.

A Writing/Citation Guide

Scott, Gregory M., and Stephen M. Garrison. *Political Science Student Writer's Manual.* 3rd ed. Upper Saddle River, N.J.: Prentice Hall, 2000.

PART 4

Writing in the Political Environment

12

Constituent Letters

Mack Mariani
MONROE COUNTY DEPARTMENT
OF COMMUNICATIONS

The U.S. Congress receives approximately 500,000 pieces of mail and at least that many emails *every week*.[1] Much of this mail comes from constituents, the people who live, work, and (let's hope) vote within a legislator's district. As you can imagine, legislative staffers have to spend an immense amount of time sorting, reading, and responding to the enormous amount of mail they receive.

Most congressional offices are simply overwhelmed by the volume of mail they receive each week. This is true (to a lesser degree) for state and local legislatures as well. As a result, virtually any intern who shows a spark of talent and enthusiasm can usually convince the legislative staff to give him or her a shot at writing a constituent response letter.

Opening the Mail

To be answered, the mail has to be opened first. Guess who gets that job? That's right—opening, sorting, and distributing the incoming mail is one of the tasks most frequently delegated to interns. Invariably you will learn to *hate* this responsibility. I know I did. You may even feel demeaned and discouraged by this duty. You may wonder (sometimes out loud), "I went to college for this?"

I have one piece of advice for you: Lighten up! Opening the mail is an important opportunity. It is not a useless job to be avoided or a form of ritual humiliation. If you are knee-deep in mail as you read this, try not to laugh. Just keep reading.

Why should you appreciate laboriously opening and sorting stacks and stacks and stacks and stacks of letters?

- *It is an important job that needs to get done.* Somebody has to do it, and frankly, given that you have only a few weeks of experience, you are probably not quite ready to draft major legislation or write a major policy address.
- *You need to pay your dues.* Most full-time staff members got their start doing exactly what you are doing. They put in lots (and lots and lots) of hours opening the mail, and typically, they still do it from time to time. Telling them that you are too good to sort mail tells the staff that you think you're better than they are. You aren't. Besides, you will never get a chance to show how great a worker you are if you don't first demonstrate that you can contribute at the most basic level.
- *Opening and sorting the mail is the quickest way for you to learn what it is your office actually does.* Sitting at your little mail station, armed with your letter opener, you will have the chance to observe all the different kinds of interactions that people have with your office. At the congressional level, this means flag requests, tour requests, casework, and other requests for assistance and letters from constituents asking the legislator to vote this way or that. You will very quickly get a good sense of what legislators and staff members actually do. Better yet, you will also figure out who in your office does what. Opening mail is the fastest way to understand your office and your colleagues and to appreciate their workloads.
- *Most important, it gives you a golden opportunity to ask for substantive work.* Take a letter from the constituent mailbox and ask your supervisor if you could take a shot at drafting a response. Of course, you should make certain that all your other work has been completed. If it is, very few staffers will turn you down.

Incoming Mail

Legislators receive a seemingly endless stream of mail, so most days the front desk is piled high with everything from letters, postcards, and petitions to directories, calendars, and slick lobbying brochures. When I worked in Washington, D.C., we once even received an apple pie in the mail as part of a lobbying campaign (we sent it back).

Advocacy/Informational Mail

Much of the mail that legislators receive comes from organized interest groups, nonprofit groups, think tanks, law firms, and other pressure groups. This mail is primarily informational and helps keep legislators and staff well informed about where different groups stand on issues of concern to the legislature. Generally, this type of mail will be distributed to individual staff members according to their responsibilities in the office. Unless you are specifically told otherwise, you should not attempt to decide for yourself which information is important and which should be thrown away. You may not always be sure who gets a particular category of mail (does information about pesticides go to the health care staffer or the agriculture staffer?). Set aside the mail you aren't sure about, and *after you are finished sorting the mail*, you can ask your supervisor for assistance.

"Dear Colleague" Letters

A "Dear Colleague" is a letter sent by a legislator to other members of the legislature. Dear Colleagues are often used to persuade legislators to support or oppose a particular issue or to bring something to their attention. In Congress, a Dear Colleague is sent internally (like an interoffice memo) and is not sealed in an envelope. The content of a Dear Colleague can include a letter, picture, cartoon, news article, or other piece of information and is sent over a legislator's signature.

Politically Sensitive Mail

Legislators are politicians. It isn't surprising, therefore, that political mailings, campaign contributions, legal documents, and other types of sensitive information are frequently mailed to their legislative offices. Federal and state laws, as well as the legislature's own internal rules, often govern the receipt and handling of political mail (particularly campaign contributions). Because the stakes are high, as a general rule you should bring this type of mail to your supervisor's attention *immediately*.

Constituent Mail

A considerable amount of the mail legislators receive comes directly from constituents. This mail generally falls into one of the following three categories:

- *Casework:* Letters asking for assistance, typically with the bureaucracy, generate casework. Most offices have very strict procedures for handling casework. These strict procedures are necessary because cases can be very complicated. Resolving a case successfully often takes from six to twelve months (two to three times longer than the typical internship). In state and congressional offices, the local or district office, where legislative staff members interact directly with the citizens and local officials who need assistance, often handles the majority of casework.
- *Requests for information:* Members of Congress and state legislators serve as a tangible link between the citizens at home and the faraway capital city. Lawmakers take great pains to respond to the numerous inquiries they receive from their constituents back home, whether those inquiries are from a student requesting information on the lawmaking process or a family requesting a map and visitor's guide to help them plan a trip to the capital. In order to facilitate a quick response, most offices will have form letters developed to respond to the most common information requests.
- *Legislative/issue-oriented letters:* Letters asking members to support an issue or asking for information on the member's position or voting record on an issue fall into this category.

Although staff can sometimes use form letters to reduce the workload, the number of issues and the variety of constituent concerns makes it necessary to constantly edit and rewrite response letters. A form letter will sometimes be appropriate when a large number of constituents sends a form letter, preprinted postcard, or petition, but an individual letter usually requires an individual response.

Outgoing Mail

Most of the outgoing mail from a legislative office falls into one of the following categories.

Constituent Mail

Letters to individuals living in the legislator's district take up a considerable amount of the staff's time and attention. Typically, these letters are sent in response to an inquiry initiated by the constituents themselves. The vast majority of constituent mail is a response to a constituent inquiry regarding casework, an information request, or a legislative issue.

Agency Letters

Legislative staff, frequently district office staff, draft letters to send to agencies, appealing for assistance in casework. These letters are typically directed to specific contact people or legislative liaisons within the executive branch agencies who are designated to work with legislative staff. A copy of the letter along with a covering form letter is typically also sent to the constituent to remind him or her that the office is working on his or her behalf.

Targeted Mailings

Legislators will sometimes select specific groups of constituents for targeted mailings. An update on legislation affecting tax breaks for small manufacturing operations might be sent to small business owners in the district, for example, since they would be the group most likely interested in—and supportive of—the legislators' position on those issues. Targeted mail can take the form of a form letter or a newsletter. The letters can be sent out to a small number or a large number of constituents. Targeted mail is very useful because it is cost effective—getting the message out to a very specific group at minimal cost. Legislators can also focus the mailings on those in the group who are registered to vote, allowing them to reduce the cost of the mailing even further.

Buck Letters and Referrals

Legislators receive many letters and emails from people who do not live in the legislator's district. Because staffing resources are stretched thin, most legislators do not respond to these letters. Instead, their staff forward these letters to the correct legislator. Similarly, legislators sometimes receive letters from people who do live in their district but regarding subjects over which they have little or no authority (for example, a county legislator receiving a letter regarding national defense issues). These letters would also be forwarded, but to a legislator or another official at the appropriate level of government.

Out of courtesy, some legislators notify the sender that his or her inquiry was received and has been forwarded ("referred" or "bucked") to someone else. The following "buck letter" reflects the format followed by one member of Congress:

Thank you for contacting me regarding [issue X]. While I would like to be of assistance to you, as a Congressional Representative I do not have jurisdiction over that issue.

It is a longstanding tradition and matter of courtesy to refer correspondence to the appropriate representative. This gives each legislator the opportunity to be of service to his or her constituents. Therefore, I have taken the liberty of forwarding your correspondence to [Person Y].

Again, thank you for contacting me. Please let me know if I can be of assistance in the future.

Writing a Good Constituent Letter: The Groundwork

Writing a good constituent letter requires some basic preparation. The first step: Ask your supervisor if you could review eight to ten letters on various topics that the office has recently sent to constituents. Here is what you are looking for:

Note the Style and Tone

Does each letter focus only on a specific point, or does it engage the constituent more broadly? Consider the tone and cadence of the letter. Are the paragraphs long or short? Is the language simple and straightforward or flowery?

Observe the Format

Forget about what you learned in high school English about the "proper" letter format. Legislators often have their own ideas of what constitutes proper format. Your letters should reflect the format that is already in place. If the paragraphs are justified, you justify. If the name is centered at the bottom of the page, then that's how it should appear on your letters too. The same goes for fonts.

Look Closely at the First and Last Sentences

Take note of the standard greeting, closing, and salutation used by your office. Most constituent letters are only four to five paragraphs long. It saves the writer a lot of time when two of the paragraphs (the first and last) are already written. This lets you focus on drafting a good response in the middle, rather than worrying about how to open or close the letter.

Ninety percent of the constituent mail that I wrote as a congressional aide started with a slightly altered version of the following paragraph:

> *Thank you for contacting my office regarding [issue X]. I appreciate having the benefit of your views on this issue.*

Likewise, my letters usually ended with the following closing:

Thank you again for contacting my office. If you have any questions, or if I can be of any assistance, please feel free to contact Mack Mariani in my office at (202) 555–1234.

Use the Standard Salutation

When you send out the number of letters that legislators do, you develop very distinct preferences about how you want your letters to read. Whether it is "Best wishes," "Yours truly," or "Sincerely," your best bet is to adopt the standard salutation used by your office and stick with it. One local legislator I worked with described himself as a "VTY guy" to emphasize that he closed every letter with the phrase "Very truly yours." This is a minor detail, but your attention to such details will allow other staff members to focus their feedback on what really matters—the content of your letters.

Use the Correct Job Title

Legislators' letters typically list a title beneath their name. Just as with the salutation, legislators will usually have a preference as to how their title appears. For example, some members of the U.S. House prefer "Member of Congress," while others prefer "Representative." Some legislators will note the number of the district ("Member of Congress—District 27") or the location (Member of Congress—Buffalo). Find out what title your legislator prefers on his or her correspondence and then use it.

Writing a Good Constituent Letter: Research

I remember when the legislative director in our office gave me my first constituent letter assignment. I took it back to my intern desk and stared at a blank computer screen for what seemed like hours. My mind raced. What should I write? How do I start? Can I really do this?

You, however, don't have anything to worry about. If you have already done your prep work (see the previous section), you should have a good feeling for the format and writing style that is already used successfully in your office. Of course, now you have to respond to the content of a specific letter. To do that, you have to know some things about your legislator and the issue of concern to the constituent. In short, you have to do some research.

First, Talk It Over

Ask your supervisor to make clear what approach you should take in the letter. Take careful notes, and if you don't understand something, ask your supervisor to clarify it!

Research the Mail Archives

Take a look at previous letters sent on that topic. Take note of any stock phrases or paragraphs that can be cut and pasted into your letter.

Research Your Legislator's Record

You probably think you know where your member stands on an issue. Use legislative research (see Chapter 9) to double-check your assumptions! You do not want to draft a letter that is inconsistent with or misstates the legislator's record. You should also use legislative research to identify past votes that can be cited as a way of demonstrating your legislator's commitment and effort on an issue.

Research Past Correspondence with That Individual

What has your legislator told the letter writer (or other members of his or her household) regarding this issue in the past? Did your office respond to a similar letter from that individual only a few weeks earlier? If so, you may want to update the constituent about any recent actions affecting the legislation. If there hasn't been any action on the issue, a shorter letter noting your appreciation for the constituent's continued interest in the subject might be in order.

Writing a Good Constituent Letter: Content

The details of a constituent letter will differ depending on the issue, the legislator, and the issue's salience. Regardless of the details, however, there are five general rules for a constituent letter's substance. Follow these rules and you will ensure that your letters are effective:

Find Common Ground

A good constituent letter reaches out to the constituent and finds common ground, even when the legislator and constituent don't agree. Make it a point to emphasize shared goals and values or to empathize with the constituent's situation or predicament.

Emphasize the Legislator's Action

A good constituent letter portrays your legislator as a person of action. Accordingly, he or she should be seen "fighting for" issues of concern to their constituents and "fighting against" efforts constituents oppose. He or she should "introduce," "cosponsor," "vote for," and "support" important legislation and "lead," "work toward," and "advocate" important goals and causes.

Claim Credit

A good constituent letter will take credit for everything your legislator can reasonably take credit for. If the legislator authored, cosponsored, or voted for a piece of legislation that subsequently became law, the letter should trumpet the role he or she played. Likewise, the legislator can take some credit if an agency takes action after he or she participated in hearings, sent letters to the agency, or otherwise pressured the agency to act.

Consider this excerpt from a letter by U.S. Representative Louise Slaughter, concerning the high cost of air travel at the airport in her Rochester, New York, district:

> *You may be interested to know that over 170 letters from Rochester travelers were included with my written comments in support of the Department of Transportation's (DOT) efforts to address exorbitant air fares paid by many fliers. The DOT has issued guidelines defining predatory practices and unfair competition practices within the air transportation industry. These guidelines respond to the national outcry over unfair competition by the major carriers, skyrocketing airfares and a lack of service for many mid-sized communities*

like Rochester. The guidelines are also called for in the Airline Competition and Lower Fares Act, a measure I am sponsoring.

Notice how this letter ties together the legislator's actions (sending written comments and constituent letters to the agency and cosponsoring the Airline Competition and Lower Fares Act) with the agency's subsequent action to issue guidelines that appear to respond to the constituent's concerns.

Although you should claim credit for whatever the legislator can reasonably claim credit for, you should also be careful not to grossly overstate or otherwise misrepresent the legislator's role. Remember how Vice President Al Gore's presidential campaign suffered for his suggestion that he invented the Internet? Don't be humble, but do keep your legislator's claims reasonable.

Build Credibility

A good constituent letter establishes the legislator's credibility either by citing his or her experience or background or by providing facts or information that demonstrates his or her expertise or understanding of an issue. One member of Congress makes it a point to include the phrase "As a former teacher and scientist . . ." in letters regarding education or technology issues. Another included the phrase "As a Member of the Energy and Commerce Committee . . ." on letters regarding issues before the committee. Phrases like this emphasize to the reader that the legislator understands the issue and speaks from a position of authority.

Emphasize the Legislator's Attention to Constituents

A good constituent letter emphasizes that the legislator is listening to his or her constituents and working to reflect their interests in the legislature.

Writing a Good Constituent Letter: Quality Control

Before you are ready to have your letter reviewed by the legislative staff, you should take some time out for quality control.

Spellcheck, Spellcheck, Spellcheck

The only thing worse than making a terrible spelling error and making yourself look bad is making a terrible spelling error and making your legislator look bad. Take the time to spellcheck your letter.

Read Through the Letter Carefully

After reading it through carefully, you should then read it again even more carefully. If you can do it without looking foolish, read it quietly out loud to yourself. Now is the time to catch any awkward grammar, typos, or spelling errors not caught by the spellcheck.

Final Words of Caution

Here are some final words of caution to help you avoid some common mistakes that can ruin your internship experience or cause harm and embarrassment to your legislator:

Resist the Urge to Rebuke Constituents

Constituents reflect the wide spectrum of human characteristics. Although the vast majority of people you will deal with are pleasant, patient, and polite, a small number will be angry, insulting, or generally unreasonable. You will be tempted to write a constituent letter similar to this now famous letter that Congressman John Steven McGroarty sent to one constituent in 1934:

> *One of the countless drawbacks of being in Congress is that I am compelled to receive impertinent letters from a jackass like you in which you say I promised to have the Sierra Madre mountains reforested and I have been in Congress two months and haven't done it. Will you please take two running jumps and go to hell.[2]*

Unless the legislator personally demands it, you should never write a letter that insults or harshly rebukes a constituent. Writing a "poison pen" letter shows a lack of good judgment on your part. If sent, it could potentially embarrass your legislator and put your internship and your reputation in jeopardy.

In July of 2001 a staff member for Minnesota governor Jesse Ventura learned this lesson the hard way. The staff member authored a constituent letter from the governor that criticized and mocked a woman who had requested assistance securing welfare benefits for her daughter. After the constituent made the letter public, the news media ran several stories about the incident. The governor was publicly embarrassed and his office was forced to apologize to the woman. The staff member, for his part, received an official reprimand.[3] Don't make that mistake.

Know When to Leave Well Enough Alone

Sometimes the most appropriate response to a constituent is to write a response that says, well, nothing. When is it appropriate to say nothing?

- When an issue is so recent or of such low importance that the legislator has not developed a stated position on the issue
- When there has been relatively little action to report on the status of an issue in the legislature
- When your office has recently responded to that individual on the same issue and there has been no change in the status of the legislation
- When the constituent is steadfastly opposed to your legislator's position on an issue and you feel there is little to be gained by engaging them directly over the issue
- When the constituent appears to be mentally unstable (trust me, it will happen)

Of course, saying nothing doesn't mean you don't have to respond. You should never ignore a constituent contact. Simple courtesy—not to mention the legislator's self-interest—requires a response. Here is an example:

Thank you very much for contacting my office regarding your concerns about daylight savings time. I appreciate your continued interest in this matter.

You can be certain that I will keep your views in mind when this issue is considered by the legislature.

Thank you again for contacting my office.

Don't Freelance

Always have your drafts approved before sending them out—without exception. The approval process gives your supervisor (or possibly the legislative director) the opportunity to see your letter before it is sent to the public. Which person is responsible for approving your draft will vary depending on the office; but every office has a policy. Be sure to follow it. Your supervisors have experience that you lack, and they will be much more likely to see problems with your letter that you might not even consider. The approval process also gives you important feedback that helps you improve your letter writing ability and better meet your supervisor's expectations.

Writing a good constituent letter may be the most important skill that an intern can master. If you can demonstrate that you can write a good constituent letter, you should expect your colleagues on the legislative staff to rely heavily on you over the course of your internship. This is good for the office, since you are an additional resource they can turn to for dependable work. It is also good for you, since it will lead to more substantive work during your internship and increase the likelihood that after the internship you will be offered a permanent staff position.

Notes

1. Helen Dewer, "Lawmakers Want Their Mail Back," *Washington Post*, October 28, 2001, A17.

2. As recounted by John F. Kennedy in *Profiles in Courage*.

3. Office of Governor Jesse Ventura, "Governor's Office Announces Discipline of Employee," press release, July 25, 2001.

Press Releases

John Czwartacki
FEDERAL EMERGENCY MANAGEMENT AGENCY

You're sitting at your intern duty station, which is about the size of your desk in third grade, when the press secretary pops her head around the corner.

"Hey, kid. You can write," she says, as a question as much as a statement.

You awkwardly nod your head.

"Wanna draft me a release?"

Now, you've written a twenty-page term paper on the social life of ants, so why does the simple request to draft a press release strike fear in your heart?

It doesn't have to.

Writing items for release to the media requires only that you know how to communicate in a style and language that your audience is used to. You do that each time you get a new professor who has a certain style that he or she demands you use. Some want everything footnoted, others want lots of detail, and still others want you to use proper grammar. And until you can meet their standards, it seems they can't understand you. The media are no different. You just need to write in a style that they understand and are familiar with.

Getting Ready

If you have an interest in writing for the press secretary, there are some things you can do before you make your first keystroke—even before you leave for your internship.

185

Read the Newspaper

Sure, there's lots of useful news and world events to learn from the paper. But it's the basic style of how information is delivered in the newspaper that can help you learn how to write for the press secretary.

Begin to read the front sections of the nation's most important newspapers—the *New York Times, Washington Post, Chicago Tribune, Los Angles Times,* and *Wall Street Journal*—not the arts and style stories, not the editorials and news analysis, but the hard news of the day. The style in which they deliver information, how facts are ordered, and how quotes are used to give texture to detail—all will help you familiarize yourself with the style in which good press releases are drafted.

Ask to See the Office's Past Releases

Read your office's old releases not just for the issues they address but also for style. You can learn about the tone and substance and how self-promoting an individual office can be in its releases, all of which will help you adjust your own writing style to the style of your Capitol Hill assignment.

Put Your Ego Aside

You may have won your high school writing symposium, gotten an *A* in Journalism 205 last semester, and have your own copy of E. B. White's *Elements of Style,* but that doesn't mean you're ready to crank out a monthly column or reelection announcement. If you do get asked to draft a release for the press secretary, expect and be thankful for lots of red marks. There's no way anyone will get the style down right away, so the edits to your work will be one of the best ways to learn the ropes of writing a press release.

The Basics of Press Release Writing

Following are some of the basic things you should know about a press release—whether you plan to write them yourself or just want to understand them better. Since media relations are an important part of how elected officials and interest groups communicate with the electorate and with other government officials, no internship would be complete without gleaning at least some exposure to this element of the job.

Audience

There are many reasons to "put out" a specific release. A member of Congress, for instance, may want to announce a town meeting, congratulate military academy appointments, or comment on a breaking news story. But there is only one goal: to inform the media of a particular fact. Only if the media fully understand what it is you're trying to say can they then in turn share your message with the public at large.

Although the media can be expected to inform the public of your announcement, town meeting, or pithy quote, you have to recognize that they are a filter—an intermediary with their own agenda, style, and needs. So a good press release needs to deliver a message that is understandable and useful to the press. You cannot forget that the primary audience for a release is the people who "buy ink by the barrel" and their colleagues in the electronic media.

A press release will be a waste of paper, no matter how important or well written, if it doesn't deliver its message to reporters in a way they can understand. You have to put yourself in the newsroom—on the receiving end of the release—when you write. There are dozens of press notices arriving in a newsroom every day or even, in the case of the national media, every hour. How to convey your information in a way that gets noticed in that environment is the challenge of the press release writer.

Who, What, When, Where, Why

Some of the most important words written by a press secretary are in the headline of a press release. Because much of how the media identifies their own work is in the form of "slugs," or short headlines, it serves you well to take a page from this way of doing business. News editors often give assignments in one- to three-word bursts (for example, "radon," "Bush speech," "tax cut debate"); photo editors label their work in a similar way; and the wire services, which provide the bulk of the reporting today, use "slugs" to identify their stories.

The press secretary's challenge is to deliver the most information using the fewest words. And it starts with the headline.

The Headline.   For example, if Representative Smith is set to speak to an American Legion luncheon where he will announce support for increasing the defense budget, your office might want to put out a news release headlined:

SMITH TO PUSH FOR DEFENSE INCREASE
AT LEGION LUNCH

Eight simple words tell the newsroom whether it's worth reading further, and they also convey almost all the general information of the release in a way reporters understand:

- The who: Representative Smith and the American Legion
- The what: An announcement for more defense dollars
- The when: Lunchtime
- The where: Wherever the legion has lunch
- The why: Although the headline doesn't specifically address this, it gives the representative a chance to explain his reasons during his speech or in the body of the release.

Five words—*who, what, when, where,* and *why*—should drive the writing of both the headline and body of the release. They also give reporters almost all the information they need to know.

The headline is also your opportunity to grab the press's attention. If there is a chance to highlight any facts that will set your announcement apart from the others flooding the newsroom, consider including them in the headline. Is a celebrity going to be at your event? Is there conflict to draw attention to? Will there be a nine-foot live ostrich in attendance? (True story—I've done it.) Any facts that can get your release extra attention should be highlighted.

The Lead.   The body of the release should be written in what journalists call "inverted pyramid" style. Simply explained, that means you want to cram some of the most important information into the beginning of the release, sometimes into the very first sentence. Subsequent sentences and paragraphs should contain progressively less critical information.

Basically you want to mirror the style of writing you see in the newspaper. Read the first two paragraphs of a story in the *New York Times*. You will see that all of the most important information of the entire story, a story that can go on for thousands and thousands of words, will have already been referenced in the story's opening.

Whereas journalists have a professional obligation to present all points of view objectively, a press secretary has a professional obligation to present his or her boss's point of view. That is why writing your release like a news story gives the reporter reading it a ready template from which to write his or her own story. By selecting for the reporter what you think are the most important facts in the form of your lead, you convey the message you are trying to deliver in a way he or she will understand, and thus perhaps influence the outcome of the story.

The lead is also a chance to call attention to the context of the subject. For example, if the announcement is a departure from past policies, here is where you want to draw attention.

Keeping with our American Legion example, a lead could read:

Representative John Smith on Thursday will address the 33rd Annual American Legion Awards luncheon, where he will announce his support for a major increase to next year's defense budget, reflecting the new requirements of national security after the terrorist attacks of September 11.

Keep it simple, keep it short, but deliver the information in a newsworthy fashion.

The Body.   The body of your release, following the inverted pyramid model, should keep the information flowing in order of importance and relevance. But just as important, it needs to be readable. Assuming for the moment that, once the news desk intern (yes, they have interns, too) takes your release from the fax machine or email inbox and it gets forwarded to a reporter—that still doesn't mean it's going to translate into news coverage for the boss.

The style has to allow the reporter's eye to move easily over your release and take in the information. Although you may have done your job and had all the most important information in the lead sentences, often there are details that can give fuller context to your announcement. One way to convey more newsworthy detail is through additional facts.

Numbers often add the detail reporters are looking for. Reporters love numbers (as long as they are accurate), and they add credibility to your release. For example, you can follow the lead above with information about the size of the boost in defense spending sought by the member of Congress, trends of growth or decline in the defense budget, or other relevant historic facts. Thus, the next paragraph could read:

Representative Smith will push for a $32 billion boost to the 2003 fiscal year defense budget, increasing overall Pentagon spending by 24 percent over the past two years. This increase will bring defense spending in line with Cold War levels as a percentage of Gross Domestic Product.

Quotes. To add a richer texture to the release and deliver reporters something they need for their own reporting, you should add a quote to the release from the member of Congress, usually by the second or third paragraph. A quote provides added color to the announcement and helps explain in the first-person voice why the announcement is being made.

It may surprise you to learn that the press secretary often composes quotes included in a news release. Then, only after it is written, does the press secretary seek his or her boss's approval. It is not practical to wait for a member of Congress to utter a phrase that's useful to a particular release. Nor is it outrageous to think that a press secretary, who often writes the member's speeches, can come up with an appropriate quote. The quote may not have been actually uttered at the time of its insertion in the release, but it will always have been approved and edited by the person it is attributed to before it is ever issued to the public.

A good quote is defined by many things: It should be short and to the point; it should take what is a complex thought and express it logically in an economy of words; and it should be something a reporter may deem interesting enough to reprint in the newspaper. In our American Legion release the quote could read:

> "We've been shortchanging our men and women in uniform too long," Representative John Smith said. "It's time we put our money where our mouth is."

The quote doesn't have to add a whole lot of new information; it simply needs to be a pithy way to express the release's point. In this case, using tried-and-true catchphrases to add some punch to the announcement of support for a funding increase.

The quote can also be used to shock, surprise, and otherwise catch the eye of a reporter. Several years ago, one congressional office issued a one-word release when a controversial cabinet official announced his resignation.

It read simply: "Good."

Because Washington often plays by very polite rules when someone ends his or her career, this biting release by a relatively unknown member of Congress caught enough attention that it was picked up by several national newspapers.

Length.   Although many releases describe very complex topics, you have to remember that the point of such a document (there are exceptions) is to give just the basic information in the most effective way possible. That means most releases are kept to one page in length. If you absolutely must write a multipage release, indicate on each page if there are more pages to follow. By tradition, the final page of a press release ends with the mark "-30-" or "###" to note that there are no additional pages.

There are times when longer releases are necessary, but you should always work to use as few words as you can to express the most information. And if dedicating only one page to the release may cheat an important issue or complex policy, there are other means to deliver the information. The full text of speeches, op-eds or guest columns, or even documents called "backgrounders" or "fact sheets" can be issued under separate covers to reporters who are interested in greater detail than a standard news release can deliver.

The reason releases are kept short is the same reason TV ads are thirty seconds: You want to get your audience just interested enough to seek to know more. If you overwhelm your audience with information, you can miss an opportunity to get the important information across.

The release's length is important, but so is the length of the individual paragraphs. If a release is just a dense pack of words on a page, it won't be read. Paragraphs within a release are usually one or two sentences long, with a rare exception made for three. You want lots of white space on the page to keep a reporter's eye moving to the important messages you're trying to deliver.

Datelines, Contact Information, and Embargo Rules.   Other key information in a news release is contained at the very top, above the headline. You may see above the headline the following:

For Immediate Release
Contact: Joe Press Secretary
March 9, 2002
(202) 225-1234

This information may seem self-explanatory, but it serves several purposes. The phrase "For Immediate Release" tells a reporter that they may use the information contained below right away. Most releases are for "immediate release," but the phrase is always included to separate them from releases that are issued under an "embargo."

Sometimes there's a need to issue a release to reporters before you wish the general public to know the information. In such cases the information is released under an "embargo," meaning reporters may begin to write their stories but may not publish the information until the time the embargo expires. For example, texts of some presidential speeches are given ahead of time to reporters so they may begin to write their reports. But they are bound by the embargo not to disseminate the information until the embargo is lifted, often the hour the speech is set to begin.

BOX 13.1 Example press release.

For Immediate Release   *March 9, 2002*
Contact: Joe Press Secretary   *(202) 555-1234*

SMITH TO PUSH FOR DEFENSE INCREASE
AT LEGION LUNCH

Representative John Smith on Thursday will address the 33rd Annual American Legion Awards luncheon, where he will announce his support for a major increase to next year's defense budget, reflecting the new requirements of national security after the terrorist attacks of September 11.

Representative Smith will push for a $32 billion boost to the 2003 fiscal year defense budget, increasing overall Pentagon spending by 24 percent over the past two years. This increase will bring defense spending in line with Cold War levels as a percentage of Gross Domestic Product.

"We've been shortchanging our men and women in uniform too long," Representative John Smith said. "It's time we put our money where our mouth is."

Smith is a Vietnam veteran and a member of American Legion Post 112 in McKee's Rocks. Smith is a member of the House Armed Services Committee and is the chair of the House Subcommittee on Military Research and Development.

- 30 -

The "contact" line in the header allows the reporter to call the correct person at the correct number for that particular release. Because the contact may be someone other than the press secretary (like a deputy press secretary), the actual contact for a particular release should be identified by name and phone number.

Concluding Words

You may not be asked to write many releases, or you may not want to. But you should at least know the basics about how your office communicates with the press. The basic skills of writing a news release will help your overall writing skills as well as give you a better understanding of how press relations work. If you have confidence in your writing skills, let the press secretary or whoever is responsible for you in the office know you're interested in trying your hand at some press release writing. Showing that kind of initiative—when it comes to writing or any other aspect of your internship—will make your entire experience all the more rewarding.

14

Talking Points, Remarks, and Speeches

Jessica Wintringham
SYRACUSE UNIVERSITY
(FORMER AIDE TO U.S. SENATOR
JOHN EDWARDS (D.–N.C.)

Politicians are criticized all the time because of the way they do their jobs. They are frequently accused of not thinking for themselves and for not being sincere. People are wary of prepared speeches and are convinced that politicians can "spin" any issue to make themselves look good. As a political intern, you will have a chance to see beyond these criticisms. One of the best ways to learn about how the legislative process works is to choose the words of a legislator.[1] It is one of the most powerful responsibilities you can have as an intern. If you write a speech to be delivered on the floor of Congress, then those words will be saved in the *Congressional Record*. If you write talking points for a meeting with constituents, then that group of constituents will go back home to their districts and share your words with friends, family, and colleagues. If you write talking points for a meeting with an interest group, then lobbyists will plan their next move based on the information that you have provided them.

One of the most challenging aspects of public office for elected officials is being held to a much higher degree of accountability than any average citizen. They are not allowed to forget a name or a face, and they must have an understanding of many complicated issues. If they tell someone they will support something and then they change their mind, when election time comes around, they are accused of "flip-flopping," or being influenced by special interests, or of being dishonest. These are just a few of the reasons why writing for legislators is such an awesome responsibility. They are held accountable for everything they say, and saying the wrong thing can hurt their career.

Writing for a legislator is a high honor and a great way to be part of the legislative process. It is a daunting task, but with some guidance it will teach you a great deal about the workings of our political system and the responsibilities of every public official.

There are four basic kinds of speech-related writing with which you may be asked to help: talking points, formal speeches, remarks, and backgrounders and briefing papers.

"Talking points" are short, generally one-page memos that staff produce to prepare legislators for interviews with the media or meetings with constituents or lobbyists. They provide legislators with prepared sound bites that summarize where they stand on an issue in one or two sentences. They often emphasize the legislator's role by pointing to specific actions they have taken to help a constituent, solve a problem, or address an issue. Talking points will also often include some background information about an issue, the legislator's voting record, or the current status of legislation. Legislators depend a great deal on talking points. This is not surprising, since they meet with so many different groups on so many different issues and do not have the time to be fully briefed before each and every meeting. Talking points are often the products of collaboration between members of the legislative staff and the press secretary or communications team. As an intern, you should not expect to prepare talking points for the legislator on your own; however, you may get the chance to help the staff by conducting legislative research or compiling information on an interest group or constituent group coming in for a meeting.

Most of the public speaking legislators do takes the form of short prepared statements made on the floor of the legislature or in committee. Most legislators are occasionally invited to make longer speeches for constituent groups, graduation ceremonies, fundraisers, public ceremonies, or other events. Prepared speeches are almost always written by full-time staff members—usually the press secretary or communications director. As an intern, you may be asked to help by conducting research for the speech or distributing copies of the speech to the media.

As public officials, legislators are often expected to "say a few words" whenever they attend a public event. "Remarks" can come in the form of a prepared paragraph for the legislator to read (a very short speech, of sorts) or a few bullet points to jog the legislator's memory. Remarks, like longer speeches, are usually put together by the press secretary or communications director.

"Backgrounders" and "briefing papers" are designed to help legislators understand the complexities of a legislative issue. Although they will often review several different sides of an issue, they are not necessarily balanced presentations. Because these materials are time-consuming to produce, the legislative staff will likely rely a great deal on the briefing materials put together by outside groups, such as think tanks, political party offices, the White House, or executive agencies. As an intern, you may help the staff collect materials from different sources or put together summaries for use by the legislator or other members of the staff.

The Many Uses of Talking Points

Talking points are used in a variety of circumstances, perhaps more often than you might expect. Every legislator is different: Some prefer to have a prepared speech for every meeting, while others need only a brief outline, even when giving a formal speech before a large audience. Most legislators fall somewhere between these extremes, using talking points several times a day and giving formal speeches only on occasion.

Luckily, a legislator's days are filled with smaller, less formal meetings, which means you could have lots of opportunities to write talking points. All legislators are different, but many of them use talking points for meetings with constituents, lobbyists, and other members of Congress. "Town hall" meetings and "listening tours" are informal gatherings designed to let the audience speak. But even when a legislator is primarily listening, he or she still may need talking points to be familiar with the issues that may come up. Constituents dislike being told that their representative knows nothing about an issue they care about, and no legislator wants to be caught off guard. Even at "meet and greets," say, a photo opportunity with a school group, legislators need to know where the group is from, why they are at the Capitol, and if they have met before.

Here is an example of talking points a legislator might use:

MEETING WITH MIDDLESEX COUNTY
PARENT TEACHER ASSOCIATION

1/16/02
2:15 p.m.
CONFERENCE ROOM

- You visited Middlesex County in April 1998 and held a town hall meeting there. You visited Green Elementary School in Middlesex County and read a story to Mrs. Brown's third grade classroom in October 2000.
- The PTA president, Maria Smith, met with your education LA last March.
- The PTA wants to talk to you about reducing class size, adding technology in the classroom, and funding school construction.
- NOTHING IS MORE IMPORTANT TO ME THAN STRENGTHENING OUR SCHOOLS.
- I MADE A PROMISE TO THE FAMILIES OF MIDDLESEX COUNTY THAT I WOULD WORK HARD TO MAKE SURE THEY HAD QUALITY TEACHERS, SMALLER CLASS SIZES, AND ACCESS TO THE LATEST TECHNOLOGY IN THE CLASSROOM.
- I AM A SPONSOR OF THE SCHOOL SUPPORT AND IMPROVEMENT ACT OF 2001 BECAUSE I THINK IT IS THE BEST WAY TO ENSURE OUR CHILDREN GET THE EDUCATION THEY DESERVE.

- MIDDLESEX COUNTY IS LUCKY TO HAVE SOME OF THE HARDEST WORKING TEACHERS IN THE STATE, AND I WANT TO CONGRATULATE YOU FOR IMPROVING YOUR MATH AND READING SCORES.
- HOWEVER, I KNOW MIDDLESEX COUNTY DE-SERVES OUR HELP. TEACHERS ARE HOLDING CLASSES IN TRAILERS, AND MOST CLASSROOMS STILL DO NOT HAVE INTERNET ACCESS.
- JUST LAST WEEK I SPOKE ON THE SENATE FLOOR ABOUT THESE IMPORTANT ISSUES, SO THAT MY COLLEAGUES KNOW THAT I WILL NOT BE SATIS-FIED UNTIL WE PASS LEGISLATION THAT IN-CLUDES MONEY FOR SCHOOL CONSTRUCTION AND A COMPUTER FOR EVERY CLASSROOM.

Work as Part of Your Boss's Memory

If you are writing talking points for a legislator, your most basic responsibility is to help her remember the issue and the audience. Most legislators know the basics of complicated legislation pretty well, but the amount of details they are required to remember about an enormous amount of issues is staggering. Some issues they discuss require them to have an understanding of science, economics, business, defense, medicine, law, and psychology, just to name a few. It is impossible for one person to remember the nuances of so many fields. Talking points are a way to simplify matters and remind your boss of the most important details concerning an issue.

Talking points can help avoid awkward situations, which is especially important if the press will be covering the meeting. A small lapse in memory on the part of a legislator can turn into a much bigger problem if it is picked up by the Associated Press or even just a local radio station. In this regard, names are very important; a failure to remember or correctly pronounce a name may make your legislator appear to be out of touch.

Write in Your Boss's Voice

Although you will most likely be an intern for a member of Congress with whom you have something in common, chances are your manner of speaking will be somewhat different. As a New Englander working for a southern senator, it took me awhile to get used to writing *y'all* in speeches. This is not a large obstacle, but it is an adjustment.

There are many ways to learn how your boss speaks. I once worked for a communications director who asked me to write down everything my boss said during events and interviews. It wasn't a fun task, but it helped me to learn his style of speaking. As an intern you most likely will not have that opportunity, but reading your boss's quotes in newspaper columns or newsletters will be helpful. Listen to him speak whenever possible. Most Congressional offices have C-SPAN on all the time, so if your boss is speaking on the floor, be sure to pay attention. Be aware, though, that a very specific language is used on the floor: the legislator probably won't speak to constituents as formally as he speaks when addressing fellow members of Congress.

While writing talking points, you should replicate the language and style of your boss as much as possible. Most legislators use certain catchphrases to capture their message or stances on issues—being aware of them might make your job easier. When your boss talks about campaign finance reform, does she talk about being "beholden to special interests?" When she talks about Social Security does she say we need to "shore it up"? An awareness of these types of phrases may help you set the tone of your talking points.

Separate Yourself from Your Boss

Writing for someone from a different background can be challenging, but it is not impossible. We spend most of our college years learning how to write in our own voice and how to express our opinions and arguments in a clear and consistent manner. We also learn how to write objectively and are taught to avoid writing in the first person in academic essays. When writing for a public official, you are being asked not only to switch off your own opinions but to take on the opinions of someone else whom you don't know very well. Naturally, it will take some effort to subdue your own opinions, especially on issues you really care about.

Even if you disagree with the stance your boss takes on an issue, you need to understand that public officials are required to make a lot of difficult compromises and to meet with people who advocate for a variety of different issues. Try to understand why your boss is taking the stance, whether it is for political, personal, or fundraising reasons. It may help you write talking points if you can understand the complexities of an issue. For example, a staff member may ask you to write talking points for a meeting with tobacco farmers, and you may be strongly antismoking. To complete the assignment in a professional manner, it is important that you separate *your* opinions on the issue from the task at hand. Remind yourself that tobacco farmers are citizens and constituents and deserve the attention of their member of Congress just like any other group. Then take a deep breath and try not to sound sarcastic while writing the talking points!

Every staffer is required to make this separation at some point, because it is just not possible to work for someone who shares all of your opinions and political ideals. You may be lucky enough to intern for someone who shares all your strongly held views, but it is very rare for anyone to find someone with whom they agree on *every* issue. If you find yourself at odds with most of your boss's most important decisions, then there is a good chance that it is simply not a good match. This experience may be difficult, but it can provide its own opportunities and learning experiences. If you decide after graduation to look for a job in politics, you might want to apply for jobs that fit your political leanings more closely.

Do Your Homework

Let's say you're writing talking points on an issue near and dear to your boss's heart. For example, your boss is going to be meeting with a group of teachers from her district about improving technology in the classroom. If it is an issue she cares about, this is probably not the first time she has spoken about it. It is worth taking the time to find out what else she has said on the issue. Her comments on the subject must be consistent. The cynics might refer to this as staying "on message," but you will learn that politicians are held to very high standards when it comes to consistency, and an innocent slip on your part could lead to accusations of her flip-flopping on the issue. So whether her campaign promises included putting a computer in every classroom or leaving technology and education to the states, you should be aware of her position when writing her talking points.

The good news about doing your homework is that it will ultimately make your job easier. If your boss has given a speech, written a letter, or made a press statement about an issue, then use these resources in your talking points. Using previously written material is not cheating in this case. The full-time staff in your office can help you find letters on almost any subject and probably can help you find information about previous meetings on the subject as well.

Use the Internet as a Resource

The U.S. Senate and the House of Representatives each have a website (http://www.senate.gov and http://www.house.gov) that has an infinite amount of useful information, including direct links to the websites of every member of Congress. State legislatures have similar sites. I urge you to spend time familiarizing yourself with your boss's website. The press office and legislative staff spend a lot of time compiling information that they think is important enough to make publicly available to their boss's constituents. Having an idea about how your boss feels on a variety of issues will give you a head start when you write his talking points. Many websites have audio and video clips, and you may even be able to listen to your boss speak about an issue just before writing about a similar or related issue.

Although every website is different, many contain press releases, columns, favorable news articles, a brief summary of the member's stances on issues, and bills he has sponsored and cosponsored. Exploring all of these categories will help you write talking points or speeches. If you are supposed to write talking points on health insurance coverage, for example, you can search all of the areas mentioned above for helpful information on the issue.

You also can use the Internet to look up information about the issue you are writing about or the group your boss will be speaking with. Many groups have a website, and a glimpse at it might inform you about their political ideology, priorities, or background. State and local newspapers also have websites that may be helpful to you. Some of them have search engines that might tell you whether the group has said anything publicly about your boss in a news article or editorial.

Understand Your Boss's Audience

You have been asked to write talking points about the Clean Air Act. Now, you may have already done all your homework and know how your boss feels about the issue and what she has said about it in the past. Your next job is to find information about the group that requested the meeting. If she's talking to an environmental group, for example, there is no need to convince them of the importance of clean air. But if she's addressing members of a corporation who are concerned with the cost of compliance, then you may want to emphasize why committing to a cleaner environment is the right thing to do.

It is also important to find out something about the relationship between your boss and the group. Did they support him in his campaign for office? Have they written any editorials praising or critiquing his performance? Have they issued any "report cards" that rate his votes on certain issues? Is this a group he speaks with regularly? If so, it might be a good idea to see what he said to them in the past (even on a different issue) to make sure the remarks you are preparing are neither contradictory nor repetitive.

Understand the Meeting's Purpose

This may seem obvious, but for a meeting to happen between a public official and an individual or group, both sides need to agree that the meeting is important. Whether the meeting is in Washington, D.C., or in the district, both parties involved need an incentive to participate. Who initiated the meeting and why? Most groups request a meeting to discuss an issue, but it might help you to know more specifically what the group's goal is. Are they looking for support? Offering thanks for past efforts? Or are they upset about your boss's position on an issue?

Perhaps it was your office that requested the meeting. If this is the case, it may give you different questions to consider. Is your boss looking for information about a topic? Is she hoping to gain their support? Do they have resources, financial or otherwise, that she is hoping to receive? Are they a link to a key constituency? Is she doing a favor for a donor or a friend?

The next piece of information that might be helpful is why both sides think the meeting is necessary. As you will find out, legislators often have staffers sit in on meetings for them because there simply is not enough time in the day to meet personally with everyone who wants some time with them. Understanding the agenda will help you prepare quality talking points. If your boss is trying to convince the group to support her, then you will want to include her accomplishments on the issue, and you should highlight her commitment to it. If the group wants her to sponsor legislation on the issue but she may not be ready to do that, then you may need to choose a more diplomatic way to discuss the issue.

Avoid Making Assumptions About Your Boss's Stances

Let's suppose you have an internship working for a member of Congress who made education one of his main campaign promises. He supports more federal funding for school construction, teacher raises, after-school programs, and hiring more teachers. You are asked to write talking points about federal standards for standardized testing. Is it safe to assume that, because of all of his other stances on education issues, he will favor this proposal? *No!* It is never safe to assume anything about a member of Congress, because what seems like a logical assumption to you may be very different from the political reality of a situation. Always question your assumptions. Though many women legislators are pro-choice, some are not. Not all legislators from the Bible Belt support prayer in public schools. If you have even the slightest bit of doubt about where your boss stands on an issue, find out! No matter how busy they are, staffers would rather answer your questions early in the process than have you rewrite talking points at the last minute.

Cover the Basics

Be sure to include the basics in your talking points, information that may seem obvious to you but may cause your boss some embarrassment if omitted. Public officials travel a great deal; they may visit several towns a day, for several days in a row. Make sure if you write, "It's great to be here," that you include "it's great to be here *in Syracuse!*" Needless to say, it would be awful for the boss to forget where she was in front of people who may be offended by such a slip. Likewise, be sure to include the name of the organization she is speaking with and any specific individuals who should be acknowledged, if appropriate.

Legislators have particularly busy schedules while at the capitol, and meetings are squeezed in between roll call votes, hearings, legislative markups, and press interviews. Transitioning quickly between groups is difficult—having a minute to read talking points can make the entry into new groups much smoother. You need to assume when writing talking points that your boss has not had a minute to think about this meeting all day. If you include information that he already knows, he can skim it and get to the new information quickly. But if he does not have the basic facts about an issue presented to him first, then the rest of your talking points might not be helpful at all. It is much safer to include the basics and risk being redundant than to skip ahead to the complexities of an issue and have it be unclear.

Vocabulary Matters

You may notice while working with politicians that, when you are introduced to them and they shake your hand, they rarely say, "Nice to meet you." Instead they often say, "Good to see you." I don't know the reason they do this, but my hunch is, although both statements convey the same message, they choose the latter because it is a warmer way to greet someone. It could also be because politicians can never be sure when they have already met someone, and it is better to play it safe than to be corrected. Either way, my point is simply that you watch not only what you say but how you say it.

Be careful with your word choices—it only takes a few words in a sentence to change the meaning of any statement. Some words make stronger commitments than your boss is prepared to make. Unless your boss has already committed to a cause, she may be meeting with a group only to assure them that she is both aware and concerned about the issues they are concerned about. Your boss may be willing to give this group her time but may not be able to make a commitment to them beyond the meeting. Make sure the language you use for addressing a group shows concern and empathy, but be careful not to guarantee any kind of action. For example, promising to look into something and promising to change something are two very different statements.

If your boss is meeting with an environmental group, your talking points should stress that clean water (for example) is a precious resource and is something that can no longer be taken for granted. You can even say that clean water is an important priority and that one of the legislator's goals is to make sure that our lakes and oceans are clean enough for our children and grandchildren. There is an important difference between these unspecific but comforting statements and promising to support or cosponsor the group's legislation.

There are other good reasons to be careful about your word choice. For example, the statement "It is so nice to talk *to* you" relays a different message than "It is so nice to talk *with* you." Although the difference may be slight, the latter phrasing can make the audience feel as though what they have to say matters and that the public official cares about listening as much as she does about talking.

Be Patient with the Writing Process

In many public offices, getting anything done can seem to take forever. You may spend all day working on talking points until you feel really good about them. You may hand it over to your supervisor with pride and then watch in frustration as it sits on her desk day after day. Then, when she finally reads it, she could ask you to rewrite it. The next time you hand it over, it may take her longer to give you feedback, and this time she might even ask others to read it. The legislative director, the expert in the issue area, and even the press office might ask you to make more changes. Don't take all this criticism personally—every staffer goes through this type of scrutiny at some point. The staff take writing for a public official very seriously, and so should you. Finding the perfect quote, the perfect way to tell an audience that you are concerned about their cause without promising to take it on, takes time and lots of practice. Enjoy each step for the lessons it offers, and don't expect immediate results.

Welcome Criticism

Interns are typically selected through a pretty rigorous application process. They are usually bright and hardworking, with high grade point averages and strong writing skills. Just as it can be hard to come from high school to college, where the expectations are often higher, it is also difficult for students to go from the college classroom to a political office. Congressional staffers have extremely high standards, and it can be difficult for interns to adjust to them.

If you are used to getting *A*s on papers, then it's hard on the ego to get talking points handed back to you covered in red ink, especially if the corrections seem trivial to you.

When I grade college students' papers, I make sure to give them both positive and negative feedback, but as a Hill staffer, I included only corrections that needed to be made. In the classroom it's my job to teach students what they did wrong and how to do better, but on the Hill it was my job to get it done quickly and perfectly. As an intern it's your job to teach yourself how to improve, and that means you need to be open to criticism that is rarely sugarcoated.

Respect the Staff's Time Constraints

I have given you a lot of questions to keep in mind while writing talking points, and I hope they will be helpful if you do not know how to begin writing or are stuck. I hope they help you with the writing process and offer you a deeper understanding of your boss's responsibilities and of the workings of political offices. But I also want to warn you against asking every one of these questions to the staffers who assign projects to you. Staffers are extremely busy, and their time is precious. If you have questions about your assignment, make sure you ask them for clarification *after* finding out as much as you can on your own. Choose a few questions listed above that interest you and that you think would be more helpful to you given the task assigned. I also advise you to use a "bottom-up" approach—don't ask the chief of staff about the public official's stance on an issue! A low-level staffer, preferably your immediate supervisor for that task, will be able to help in most cases and will have more time to work with you if you need help. Because they focus in more depth on fewer issues and because they communicate with constituents regularly, those staffers will be a great resource to you.

This may seem like common sense, but just to remind you—timing is everything. Don't ask for help from a staffer when he is on his way in or out of the office, is on the phone, or seems stressed or frazzled. You might ask when he'll have time to answer some of your questions or even send him an email with a list of your questions so he can answer them when he has a minute between meetings, while on hold, or another such time. My experience has been that the more respectful you are of staffers' time, the more willing they are to spend it on you. A good relationship with staff will provide you with a more meaningful internship experience, not only because you'll learn more but also because they'll be more likely to write you positive recommendations and maybe even keep you in mind for future job opportunities.

Technicalities

As you begin to pay attention to the finishing touches of your talking points, don't forget about format. Make sure you find out what size font your boss is comfortable reading and how she wants the sentences spaced. Does she want a summary or does she want the speech written out word for word? If a summary, does she want a page of bullet points, and do the points need to be in complete sentences? Does she like to have the group's name and interest written in a different color? These may seem like trivial details, but you would be surprised how much trivial details matter in the political world!

Be Ready for Any Learning Experience

Every political internship is different, and there are no guarantees about the different assignments that may come your way. Not every intern gets the chance to write for his or her boss, and those who do may not be excited about the issue, the group, or the part of the task they are assigned. You may feel at times as if you're doing busywork or that your task is tedious or unimportant. When you're busy wondering why you're spending your summer working for free in a stuffy office instead of lying on a beach, remember two things. First, in political offices, there are no unimportant details. Details can make or break reelection campaigns, fast-track or derail key pieces of legislation, and patch together or drive apart important alliances. The time you spend on details saves the staff, and ultimately your boss, a lot of problems in the long run, and even if they don't say it often enough, they are grateful to you.

Second, every seemingly tedious task has a lesson to teach you, usually a lesson that you wouldn't learn anywhere else. Spending all day putting together talking points for a five-minute meeting might seem a waste of your time, but it helps a public official do her job and improves the relationship between your boss and the audience. It gives you a chance to learn about the office's responsibilities and about what is expected from you. Writing for a public official might help you decide for yourself whether Americans are right to be cynical about the motives of politicians or whether our representatives are working hard to improve the lives of their constituents. Either way, your conclusions will be based on firsthand knowledge that can only be gained from being part of the process, and that, I hope, will make the less glamorous parts of your internship seem worthwhile.

Note

1. I am writing based on my experience in Congress, but what I say in this chapter applies to almost all public officials, whether legislative or administrative.

PART 5

Last Words

15

The Interns Speak

Grant Reeher et al.

In the fall of 2001 Grant Reeher conducted two focus groups with Syracuse University undergraduates who had recently completed a broad range of internships, including placements on Capitol Hill and in congressional district offices and with interest groups, local and national political campaigns, state representatives, law enforcement organizations, and media organizations covering politics. Several of the students had past experience in two or more internships. The students were kind enough to sit down and share their thoughts about their experiences. The following material is a merged and edited transcript of those two conversations.

The students participating in the groups were Beth Breuer, Karen Brown, Eric Colchamiro, Michelle Elias, Jennifer Gagliano, Joyce George, Laura Gottlieb, Kate Hall, Leah Hoffman, Diane Ibrahim, Bert Kaufman, Boris Milgrom, Aaron Panzer, Jenna Pantel, Gideon Rafel-Frankel, Stephanie Roehl, Tim Schlittner, Natalia Swalnick, and Jason Volack. In order to protect both the students and the organizations for which they worked, we have substituted generic labels for proper names where appropriate. These substitutes are placed within brackets.

What's the most important piece of advice you would give to an intern about to start in a political internship?

Bert: You've got to be prepared to do a lot of grunt work, some menial tasks, but also, don't be prepared to do only that. I think part of what makes a good internship is the experiences that you have available to you, aside from the grunt work—like actually working on policy or press releases, things like that. And getting a certain amount of interaction with the boss, so I think that if you're stuck in an internship where you're doing nothing but grunt work, I think you should stand up and say something to the intern coordinator.

Laura: I totally agree with that. You go into the internship thinking that it's all going to be glitz and glamour, and you're going into politics, and you're going to be doing all the exciting stuff, but don't be dismayed if you do find yourself doing the menial tasks of copying and stuffing envelopes and filing and that kind of stuff. That shouldn't be all the internship, but don't be dismayed if that's part of it.

But also don't be afraid to step forward and ask for more to do. Oftentimes they forget that you can get things done quickly and are just as efficient as they can be. They give you a task and you finish it, and then you sit there with nothing to do. So, don't be afraid to put yourself out there and just ask for more to do if you're looking for that extra step.

Leah: I'd say that being an intern isn't simply nine to five, or whatever hours you have. If you want to get out of the grunt work, then you have to do the research, you have to keep your eye on the media [or] your representative, if you're working in a representative's office; then you're also the eyes and ears of that representative. You can just have like a letter, a little memo each day, like this just sort of came up, I just wanted you to know— or ask some questions. It shows that you're thinking about it, and it's not just when you give me a project, it's "I have a project—I just need you to okay it." People always like to okay things and get credit for it.

Jason: Don't let your internship immediately become you serving some-body else's interests. You have to go in knowing what you want to get out of it, and know who works there and know what your office or your company does, because that allows you then to ask questions to the people who work in your office. If you don't ask questions, they think you're happy and that you are content with doing what they want you to do. But if you go the extra mile and handle what they're handling, they're more than happy to teach you what they do, because people love to talk about themselves and their job, and they'd be more than happy to talk about what they do and how you could do it, too.

Eric: I think one of the biggest things to note in terms of taking the initiative and knowing what people do is translating that into building relationships with the people who already work there. I mean, one of the smartest things, at least from my perspective, that I did on one of my internships was, one day we were talking in the office about a basketball game that was occurring that evening. The tickets were only five dollars, and I was already going down there with my dad to go to the game. But when I got down there to get tickets, there were two extra tickets, so I called the chief of staff in our office—I called him from the basketball game—and I offered him the tickets, and he came right down. And from that point on, you could see a considerable difference in our relationship. He was more friendly to me, he started assigning more things to me, and he just had more of a trust in me. And I think that's an important thing to know, under the whole theme of the internship not being only a nine-to-five thing, because that can also pay off in the future.

Gideon: It's so important to find a mentor in the office, even if they're not in your department, even if they're not your direct boss—someone who not only that you talk about office things but, like Eric said, you can talk about anything, and which will keep you up-to-date, especially if you're working in [a large organization]. When you're just an intern on one floor, [you're] not really knowing so much of what's going on on the other floors. I became really good friends with the internship coordinator, so he was able to keep me attuned with what was going on with the other interns on the other floors, what was going on between the staff on the other floors. Now that I've left, I can have a correspondence with him about the campaign, [the organization's initiatives], about job opportunities, about other things. And he knows me, and he loves me, so it's not like just emailing your boss, who's real busy and who is getting all these emails from hundreds of interns. He's probably getting a few from a few people who were attracted to him and who took a friendship to him and he took a friendship to them.

And the other thing I would say is passion. I really didn't know much about [the organization] before I started interning there—I kind of fell into that internship. But I acted like [its areas] were my life. I'd read the books that they gave me, read the handouts that they gave me, and I went around acting like I was an advocate [for that cause] for many years. And I think that's important because a lot of the interns there were advocates for many years, a lot of them were doing [related activities] and were doing their summer thing there. It was important for me to be on the level with my peers and act as dedicated—and for that summer I *was* as dedicated— but act as dedicated and talk as dedicated as they were.

I also have a caveat. Learn to keep your mouth shut at certain times. You know, you do hear some things that should basically stay in the office or should stay between you and another person. You should keep that quiet because basically loose lips do sink ships and could hurt your career, because it does damage the trust if they find out.

Stephanie: An intern has to learn to keep their mouth shut, because you'll get into a lot of trouble if the media hears anything that you say. I heard about some girl who got a job in my old office, and she just got fired for opening her mouth, so that's a big one.

Do your work and get to know [the staff]. Try to get to know them, and you'll get good recommendations afterwards, and you'll have a better time at your internship.

Tim: I would give two pieces of advice when taking on your internship. My first is to be patient. Like as others said earlier, you will be doing menial tasks. You're not going to go into your internship on the first day and they're going to say, "Hey, intern, go write a health care bill for us." They're going to actually have you doing stuff that they need done right away. But if you're patient enough and you persevere through these tasks and you do them well, then as time goes on you'll start to get more important things, you'll start to be more in the loop of what's going on in the office.

My second piece of advice would be to be pesky and annoying. Say, "What can I do for you, what are you doing today?" Talk to the legislative director: "What's going on today's agenda, can I help, can I do this, can I do that? Is there anything I could possibly add today to make your job a little easier?" And you know what? The first three times, the first five times, they might be like, "No there's nothing you can do; please go back to answering phone calls." And you do that. But if you persevere, and you persist, and you keep doing that, they're going to see in you that drive to do something well and to be part of the power in Congress and the work.

I think that will reward you if you continue to show that kind of persistence in the office. I know personally it rewarded me, by being that pesky annoying kid that wanted to do things more than the other interns.

My desk where I sat was right in front of a legislative assistant who's in charge of a set of issues, and I hear what he's doing everyday. And I'd just walk back to his desk and we'd talk about the issue. And I'd say, "You know, I'm interested in doing this; this is how I feel about things." And he's like, "Yeah, okay, you know, I can't really help you right now." But as time went on, in this seven-week internship, things like [the boss] was away for a trip, and they were debating a constitutional amendment to ban flag burning, and he had to make a speech—this was very important to him, because he had a lot of veterans in his district. So he had to write a speech . . . that would be published in the *Congressional Record.* So this legislative assistant comes up to me and he goes, "Why don't you write it." He had heard me being interested in writing and doing stuff on the issues, so I wrote it. The next day I opened the *Congressional Record,* where some of the most powerful people in history had written, and I see the speech I had written, and then I knew it was worth taking all those phone calls.

Michelle: I totally agree that you have to take the initiative and show them that you want to be there even if you really don't know what's going on. Put a smile on your face, go in early, stay late. I made it a point when I worked to, before I left, go to the chief of staff and ask, "Is there anything else you need before I go?" And oftentimes the other interns that worked with me, if they had free time, if there was nothing to do, they would just sit there. They'd sit at the desk, answer the phone, whereas I would ask, "Is there anything else that I can do?" Part because I wanted to help and then part because, too, that I would benefit from it rather than just like sitting there reading all afternoon.

Jenna: Stay active. I know a lot of the time they'd give me a project and I would finish it earlier than they expected. Just follow up on it and like try to keep on asking for more, because it shows that you're interested in expanding your responsibility in that way. You seem like you're not being lazy and just waiting for them to give you something.

Natalia: I think that if you see something [interesting] going on in the office, act like you're really interested. And if you've already proven that like you can handle basic office tasks, just mention that you're interested in working on the project. They're more likely to let you jump in if you're proactive.

Diane: I think if you're starting out doing very little, like things you don't think are necessary or you don't enjoy, I'd just go along with it—wait a bit until you gain a trust with your intern supervisor, and then he'll move you on to larger tasks that might be more important. They're not going to trust you with them right off the bat. They're going to see exactly how you work, what skills you have, and if you do things correctly and as they ask. So if you start off photocopying, photocopy. And be happy about it.

Laura: Again, about building relationships, internships aren't just about experience; they're about connections. And if you're in the field that you want to go into eventually, find out the people you're working for—who do they know? Or if you have to make a phone call to do a project, strike up a relationship with this person. Those connections that you make will eventually help you get a job in the future, will help you get into grad school, will help you get that fellowship that you're looking for. So the connections that you make while you're there are so important to your future career.

Bert: To add on to what she said, it's very important not only to develop relationships with people in the office, but also outside the office, other interns. You know, I met a lot of other interns from other offices, different parts of the country, and also lobbyists—especially if you're in Washington, they're everywhere. And we got taken out to lunch and to fundraisers and things like that, and that's another way to get to meet people. But also, I think it's another big thing to meet other interns from other parts of the country. I can't tell you how many people I ran into that expressed hopes of becoming the next senator from Colorado or president. There's definitely so many people who have a lot of future political aspirations that probably will get to achieve that.

Jason: I really think when they hire you as an intern, it's kind of like a trial run for a real job, so it's important to explore your internship and to be annoying to ask for a task. But when you do get a task, don't just complete it. Complete it to the best and absolute top of your abilities, because that determines the next task that you're going to get. And if you've completed it to the best of your abilities, and they find it amazing, they're going to give you the best job the next time around.

Aaron: Be on time. Don't slack off at all. I mean, they don't like it if you show up even five minutes late. Don't say, "I can only work like a minimal amount of hours." Be open to what time you can work. Especially when you're working with the public, you have to always be cheerful, even if it's something that you really don't want to do. For instance, when I worked on the campaign, when I went out door-to-door campaigning, if I walked around with a mean look on my face, that would get the voters pretty angry, and we might lose their vote. I had to walk around, be cheerful, even when people would slam the door in my face, because they're like, "You're helping out a Democrat; we're Republican." I still had to put a cheerful look on my face. Most of the time people would want to talk to you even if it wasn't about the campaign. I had some nice ladies that would talk to me for about fifteen minutes, and they're giving us their support just because you were so nice to them.

Jennifer: I think that one of the important things is to know what sort of program you're going into, like if it's one that's very well structured, or if it's very free and it's kind of like fend for yourself. Knowing that going in; it will give you an idea of just how enthusiastic and how open and how pushy you have to be in the internship—whereas if you're entering an already very structured internship program, they're going to have a lot of plans and tasks for you already assigned that they're going to want the interns to do, and they may not want you to step out of that. So it really helps to have some sort of idea of what you're going into.

Diane: I think that it all depends. I think you should feel out what atmosphere an internship has before you can tell a person exactly what to do and what not to do. Only because, I think, that some internships may be more of a casual atmosphere where you can work with your supervisor to do whatever it is that you would like to do, and I think other internships might be a little bit more structured. I mean, basic things like being on time, things like that, you need to make sure that you do, just as though you were working in an actual job.

Karen: Even before you get the internship, you want to make sure that you're somewhat interested in the field, because your ambitions reflect how you're going to be in that office. If you're really excited about going into the internship, you'll do well, because you want to be there. So don't choose something that you're just doing because it will look good on your résumé.

Everything I've heard so far sounds pretty good. I want to hear some of the bad stuff. What bad experiences have you had? I'm also interested in hearing observations of somebody else's internship in your office, or in another office, that went bad, and why.

Michelle: When I went to D.C., I was going for the semester through [a university program]. I had a huge book of internships, and I applied, but I found this one. They were going to pay me. I interviewed over the phone, did the whole writing sample, et cetera. So I was excited; I'm ready to go. But the guy who was the executive director—I was getting some weird vibes on the phone—where he called me once at night, like really shady kind of, you know, inappropriate thing. So you know me, I'm all going to D.C.; I've got my pride, I'm going. So I get there, and my parents do the whole Metro thing. And it's literally in an alley; it's literally like a shanty—I took pictures, and it was like, the sign was carved out of wood. These guys are telling me how they have like bills in Congress, et cetera. My parents are like, "You know we don't really feel comfortable—it's in an alley." But I didn't tell them about the phone call, so I go back, and I don't know what to do. It's my final decision, and I called the director of the [university] program and told him I was having some apprehensions. I'm a little nervous, uncomfortable. He said you have to, if you feel that vibe, then don't be too proud. Stop, call, and say you can't go, because it's not worth feeling uncomfortable for an entire semester in doing something that you don't love.

Jennifer: I would say I went into my internship expecting that it was a very structured program. That I was going to move from department to department, doing a little bit of everything with some of the [different departments]. This was my impression of what it was going to be like. I ended up going into [a particular division], and basically we played catch-up the whole semester with the person who was in this department, because she was very much behind in what she had to do, and therefore it was a lot of me opening files, preparing letters. I would say that I worked basically like a paralegal. I did most of the things that all the paralegals were doing. I would say that I had substantial tasks to perform, but I never did have the opportunity to work with the other divisions, which is what I had been wanting to do. I was especially interested in [another department] because . . . the focus I want to end up taking is working with the FBI. So I was very interested in [that department], but I wasn't able to break into that.

Joyce: I worked for [a] senator. I think [the senator is great], and I worked for the fundraising committee. I wouldn't put [the senator] down. I spent the whole summer doing the fundraising, which is really cool for the department because we were pretty much bringing in all the money for the campaign. [The senator] always has a thing like, "Ah, my interns," and all this stuff. But we never met [the senator] at all. I remember that [the senator traveled] for a fundraiser, and the internship director called me and told me to go and help out. We went there and it was good seeing everybody from the office. We went to go take a picture with [the senator]. The internship director said, "This is Joyce, she worked in our office fundraising department." And the reception that [the senator] gave me, [the senator] was carrying on, "It's so nice to see you again! How have you been?" and blah, blah, blah, like we were old friends. I was like, "This is the first time I'm meeting you." I just felt so—just this whole level of fakeness. I was really just dismayed by that.

   On the other hand, I had an internship experience with [a different senator]. I thought [this senator's] going to be like a stuck-up [person], not going to fiddle-fuddle with the interns in the office. But [the senator] comes [out to the district office] every month and sits with you, has lunch with you. [The senator] was giving me advice on telling my mom about the Atkin's diet, so [the senator's] like this down-to-earth [person]. So you go in there with this expectation, and it can go in both directions.

Leah: I was with [a presidential] campaign during the primary season in New Hampshire. To give a little background, I was [torn] between [two candidates]. I don't know which one I want. I looked at the two programs. [One] had a sheet like, this is when you can be working, this is what you can be doing—it was specifically there. [The other campaign] is like, oh, just send a fax and then we'll be fine. [The first] campaign had more structure, and that was what I was looking for.

I got there. Everyone's not familiar with New Hampshire—I wasn't either, and I got lost a lot. I was based in Claremont, New Hampshire, which is thirty minutes away from the border with Vermont. They gave me housing in Vermont—I drove to Claremont—but every night we would have to go to Manchester for some reason, which is in the bottom of the state. Then we had to go to the seacoast. I spent most of my time driving. During that week, I went over one thousand miles in my car, and I spent most of my time in the car.

Our office got closed because we had gotten permission from the person who owned the office to use it, but he decided—because he's a supporter [of a different candidate]—he's like, "Oh, I didn't realize you'd be using the phone." And we got kicked out. And so that was the end of my internship, because we got kicked out. It was crazy.

I know that campaigning is supposed to be [difficult]—you're into an office. If you're campaigning and you stick with them, then you become part of the foundation. But I don't think I learned that much. Basically the biggest lesson I learned was it's hard to campaign.

Karen: I would come in every week like at a certain day, around a certain time. And it seemed like every time I would go in there, they'd be like, "Oh you're here; let's find something for you to do." That's how you end up with copying stuff and filing.

Stephanie: My friend worked for [a senior senator] and had the worst experience of her lifetime. And the only reason why she worked there is because [the senator] was [well-known]. She was just doing stuff—they didn't appreciate her—she was doing stuff that was just ridiculous. She sat way in the back with no windows in the mailroom for a whole semester, opening up mail that was dated since the beginning of that summer. And we were in spring semester. Whereas I worked for a freshman [member of Congress], and I felt very comfortable with the interview and very comfortable with the office and had an awesome experience. I researched cases, I wrote in the *Congressional Record* and wrote for the [member] when [the member] spoke on the floor. I worked with constituents and stuff like that. So it was a lot different for me. I got a lot more experience.

Diane: Make sure that you have long-term projects so that there's always something you can go back to. One day my immediate supervisor wasn't there, and no one really knew what to have me do. So the secretary decided that I was going to clean out the closet, and the closet was probably half the size of this room. I was all dressed up nice for my day at work and covered in dust, climbing up ladders trying to take things off shelves—it was horrible. So a long-term project is a good thing.

Natalia: When I worked at the [state capitol], there was an intern the summer before—he didn't really like his internship. He was in his legislator's office, and he was listening to the radio and they were having a call-in show, and they got on the topic of worst jobs ever. And the intern called up and said, "Oh yeah, I'm working for State Representative so-and-so, and they have me doing this, this, and this." And other people in the capitol were listening to the same radio station and heard that. And they told the representative, and the representative fired the intern.

That would do it. How about stories, either about yourself or others, where you started off doing less interesting things but were able to work your way to doing more interesting, substantial things? How does that work?

Stephanie: I worked my way up to writing a speech for a press release. [When I started,] it was like clippings and stuff like that and basic intern responsibilities, copying. And then I started helping out the speechwriters, and then they allowed me to write my own press releases. I just did my job, and talked to the people, and started talking to the speechwriters and going to their desks and asking them for advice or just talking to them in general. Small talk. I was doing my job, and it was my internship advisor who said, "Go ahead, write a press release—you're ready."

Laura: At [an interest group] office in D.C., although some of the stuff was very interesting, a lot of the stuff I did every day was photocopying and cutting out clips from the newspaper that were relevant to what we were talking about at the time. That was a lot of my day and a lot of the first few weeks. But toward the end of the internship, as things were getting crazy—it was [the] 2000 election year, and [the group] puts on a lot of events at the Democratic and Republican conventions. Towards the end I started getting more involved with planning for these conventions and helping get needed signatures, helping plan for these programs. I ended up going to the Republican convention with [the group]. This was the last week of my internship, and by this time the staff, the political staff, got to know me a lot more and trusted me a little bit more, and specifically [the group] hired five interns to just work at the Republican convention, whereas I had been working all summer at the office. The staff knew me more and gave me the tasks instead of giving it to the new interns. I was sitting at the table checking in ambassadors and senators for the event, and I got to go have lunch at [a senator's] house, and I got to help out at the congressional breakfast the next morning. So by this time they trusted me more as opposed to, the beginning of the year I was just doing a lot of the copying. The last week of the internship, at the convention, they were giving me the tasks that they really needed to get done.

Tim: On Capitol Hill, a lot of times the intern coordinator is also the office assistant—I know that's how it worked in my office. And as someone described earlier, the office assistant is basically the secretary. Their jobs are answering the phones, sorting the mail, getting faxes to the proper people. And as an intern, when you're going in and you're new, you go to the intern coordinator for work. Now, the intern coordinator is giving you the work that he or she needs to be done, which is office assistant work. So if you continue to go to the intern coordinator, which I did for the very beginning, and ask them for work, you're going to continue to sort post-cards, or different faxes, or taking issue papers and giving them to the proper legislative assistant. And I did that and I did it for so long before I was like, I do not want to read another Social Security postcard that says I want my benefits, or some NRA postcard that ten thousand people sent in saying, "I want to carry my firearms in the supermarket."

So finally—and I said this earlier—I decided to go to other people in the office. And that's where the change was. Going to the legislative assistant, going to the legislative director, going to the chief of staff, and saying, "You know, I'm glad to be here; I'm glad I could help out in these areas with the intern coordinator, but I want to get something out of this. I want to do these things; this is what I'm interested in." And if I hadn't actually stepped away from the intern coordinator and went and branched out to other parts of the office, then I would have had a miserable seven weeks answering calls about Gary Condit.

It sounds like, for some of you and to some degree, there's also a bit of luck or chance involved in getting the better tasks.

Michelle: When I got to the Hill, my [member of Congress] was put on [a committee], and our staff assistant moved up to the committee with some legislative assistants. So his office was kind of left in shambles. When I get there, they're like, "Normally you'd be doing this, but we have no staff assistant." I got there first in the morning, I took the papers out, I checked the voice mail, I photocopied Roll Call and put everything out. I guess because I was the first intern there, because I was there for a whole semester, they were like, "Oh, Michelle can do it." It wasn't bad, because I kind of like administrative tasks. But there's only so much you can staple, having to run the office, and [greet] every constituent that walks through the door, schmooze with them, make them feel comfortable, and listen to some woman complain or yell at you because she doesn't like the way the [member] voted, tell you that you're wrong for working in his office because he supports abortion and God is going to strike you down—that kind of can be overwhelming. But then it did get better because like, as time passed, we got a new staff assistant and she took over more of that stuff, and I got to work on legislative stuff.

Jenna: My first day on my internship, I started with the county manager, and he wasn't there, but they gave me reading on tobacco policy; and the next day I was to start writing a primer on it. So my first three, four weeks at my internship, I had a lot of responsibilities there. I wrote a whole primer, which I understand they're handing out to people in the state. With the legislator, I worked with redistricting and stuff like that, so I was given a lot of responsibility. And then I moved downstairs in the office to

real property tax. It was much different; I felt that I was doing more secretarial stuff. So I think it depends where you are. And then I went back
up later to the legislator's office, and they gave me minor tasks, not as big
as [at] first. They didn't have as much time to pen something out for me.
Then I ended up doing secretarial work, so it kind of went backwards.

*There are a lot of interesting themes coming out of everything all of you are say-
ing; one I hadn't thought about in the context of internships is the importance of
finding a mentor. But I want to probe something else. It seems that there's a premium you're placing on being somewhat "entrepreneurial" in getting better
things to do, being proactive and at times even aggressive or assertive. But at the
same time, you need to be patient and do the mundane work well and with a good
attitude. So there's a navigation of those two—almost like your internship is a
living organism, and you need to make sure it goes through a metamorphosis
from caterpillar to butterfly. And you can't try to change over too soon, or you'll
alienate people. How do you navigate all this?*

Natalia: I think if you ask in a positive way, if you're seeking work—not
like you don't think that they're giving you work. If you say, "Don't you
have any *work* for me to do?" I think that's negative, and they're not going
to look upon you favorably. But if you're like, "Oh, I finished this task, is
there anything else you need me to do before I leave?" or "Is there anything you need me to do to work on long term?"—if you try to act like
you're seeking work, instead of looking down on them for not giving you
work, I think that they're a lot more receptive. Don't seem like you're
complaining and whining—act like you're seeking out more work to do
because you want to help out more.

Kate: I think it's really important to use your brain. It sounds kind of simple, but it seems like, if you get caught in the everyday run of things and you
just keep going along with the flow, you're going to be stuck there. I know
in my situation working for the campaign, I would think about the choices
they were making for the campaign and what I thought, like they wanted to
do this piece with their opponent. If you can bring them something different, that they didn't otherwise think of, I think they might actually look to
you for something, versus just give you the stuffing of the envelopes.

Aaron: I think also you should always use manners. Always say "please," "thank you," "you're welcome." People that you're working for love to hear that, and that might help get you through to doing some better stuff. Also they might say, "Oh, this is a good kid." If it involves working with people outside the office, they'll say, "Oh we can send this kid to do something because he'll be polite."

Diane: You should also take note of different personalities within one office. Even if the structure's all going to be one way, there's different personalities and you should take note of who you think you can go to to ask for those more important tasks. There were certain [staffers] that I might not have felt comfortable going and having a regular conversation with, and there were other [staffers] that I was very comfortable with. So when I was looking for tasks, I would go to one I was comfortable with. Because they trusted me more—we had better rapport—they would give me better tasks.

Jenna: Dress professionally and act professional. You just have to show them what you're capable of.

Gideon: It's important not to be fake. I mean, Eric talked about shaking hands and all that stuff. It's important, but I think it's important not to be fake. If you go in there on the first day, think you're hot shit, you're going to piss people off. Be yourself. No one on the first day of a job is going to go in and act like they know everything. In searching out all the mentors and searching out everyone that's going to make your internship a great experience, be yourself because, if you're not yourself, I don't think you can have a good experience even if you're doing the most amazing thing.

Michelle: I just wanted to follow up what Gideon said about not being fake, and what we said about asking questions. I think that's so important, because everybody goes down there like with the idea, I'm this overachiever, and I'm going to do the best job I can, and they're going to offer me a job. Don't psyche yourself out and be excessively . . . it's okay to make mistakes, they know you're human. They're not expecting interns to be like these machines. If you do make like an error, obviously apologize and catch it in the future. But don't be so freaked out that you can't tell them that you made this mistake, because everyone's human.

Tim: I just wanted to comment on what you said before about striking a balance. I think the best metaphor is, it's like being on a sports team. You come up, you pay your dues, you watch the other more experienced veterans play, you learn, and then it's your turn. And you have to pay your dues. You can't come in and expect to step into a high-profile position, because that's not how it works. Politics is a profession where there's stepping stones and you really have to just focus yourself on learning from others. I mean, George Stephanopolous was a Richard Gephardt intern. That was one of his first jobs, so I think in the office just pay your dues, show them that you care. And like Gideon said—I agree—don't be fake. Don't ask questions that you really want to sound smart asking the questions. Ask the questions that come to your head. Ask the questions you're curious about, and they'll appreciate that and eventually you'll be moving up and doing the stuff that they do. But it's not—it's a gradual process, like you said.

Bert: Unless you don't want to get into the game. There were a few interns in our office, actually one, who was a major problem, who took up a computer all day and just emailed his friends and talked on the phone.

We're not writing the book for that—don't worry. So what I'm hearing is that the way to thread this needle is to strike a combination of good attitude, hard work, show up on time, pay attention to what's going on around you, and when the opportunities come, be ready for them. Develop personal relationships whenever possible—but I want to come back to an aspect of that. Having said all that, also some of this is going to be determined by the office itself, structurally. Not to turn this too much into an academic subject, but there's an external structure that is beyond any individual's control. But within the contours of that structure you can change outcomes by what you do. And asking and being polite and helpful, all are factors to help the outcome be a good one.

Two final questions. The first one is—and you've already spoken to this a bit—the relationship between the internship and future employment. Have people here established real contacts that could lead to future jobs? Has anyone here probably gotten a job, you think, from the internship?

Tim: The internship I did after my freshman year. I interned there, I worked on his campaign. And I've already been—I've been talking to the chief of staff—and they've indicated to me that they'd be interested in having me do something in communications. They know I'm in [the communications program] here. So I think that's been established.

Bert: My desk was right in front of the office manager, who was responsible for all of the hiring. She happened to be from upstate New York too, so there was some connection there, and she said to keep in touch with the office, and "I think we'd be interested when you get out of college."

Joyce: I've been able to keep in touch with the legislative coordinator, and we're really close. She said, if I wanted to take a year off before I go to law school, they need an intern coordinator, someone who knows the ins and outs of the office really well. They keep asking me to stay with them and work with them.

Michelle: For [a government department], my boss told me that—there was another woman from Syracuse, too—he likes how we worked and what we did so well that he said that he'd be willing to help us. He's got a lot of [department] connections.

Jason: Well, when I was finishing, they didn't say directly "come back, we'll have a position for you." They did say that they would be hiring for the 2004 campaign, when I would be graduating. Also, there are certain companies that just hire interns. There are certain agencies or organizations that are big enough, that have a big enough turnover, there's jobs open for young people. And they tend to give them to interns.

Stephanie: Keep up with your contacts. If you worked for someone, keep in contact with them. Give them a call. If you're in the area, go visit them. I was working for [a party congressional office], which is right next door to the representative's office where I also worked at. So I visited them over the summer several times. I called Washington a lot and talked to them. While I was there, I found out that we all enjoyed baked goods, so I just sent them baked goods to keep up with them, to keep them remembering who I am. When I go to D.C. sometime next semester I'm going to go visit them. So keep in contact with them. Or especially if you go to committee meetings or you're introduced to someone, get their card and introduce yourself. And if you have a card, give them your card, so that you can use those down the line. Say, "I met you during this committee meeting when the Congressman introduced me to you. I was an intern at the time. I was just wondering if you'd help me do this."

Final question. One of the things that has come up here is the importance of interpersonal connections—schmoozing, demonstrating interest, striking up conversations, staying in contact. One of the concerns for a lot of people—especially women—is personal safety and psychological safety. Am I going to end up in a situation where I could be compromised? It's a difficult situation. Washington has a lot of young, single people in it. What advice would you give to someone to navigate that tension?

Stephanie: Especially in D.C., the power—it's almost like you feel the power. Everyone around you knows someone who knows someone who can put you to the most powerful office in that area. And you have to watch it, because they're going to try and abuse their power—there are going to be some people who will. If something like that happens, especially for girls, don't be afraid. Be polite about it, but in the same sense be firm in the way you're talking. Say they make a pass or something. Say, "This isn't appropriate, and I'd appreciate if you just don't do that again. Don't speak in that manner, and don't touch me that way." If it continues, you're going to have to do something a little bigger, but hopefully addressing it immediately—and politely but at the same time with a firm tone of voice—hopefully it'll stop. And don't be afraid by the power.

Kate: I think it's really important to try to prevent that before it happens, too. There are ways to go about that, like your way of dress. Dress appropriately, not so that you're trying to get people interested in you. Also the way in which you show interest in that person is really important. Make sure it's clear that you're interested in what they're doing, not them themselves, their own personal lives. I think those are kind of important in terms of preventing it from getting to that point. If it does get to that point, I go with what you're saying. Be clear, exactly.

Natalia: If someone starts getting a little more personal and familiar with you, keep professional. Don't start talking about your boss's marital problems with them or something like that. The next thing, I think they go up a scale, like the really uncomfortable stuff will, I imagine. But I would think there would be maybe a couple of warning signs that there's an attraction there, before something that makes you very, very uncomfortable would come up.

Gideon: Don't let fear paralyze you. I think some interns let it paralyze them. Go around, definitely go around with a friend. Have a partner in crime that you hang out with. If you go to someone's house for dinner or you go out to a bar, have a girl or a guy friend with you, that you are both going home to the same place. If you're going late at night—but I think it's like a lot of other things. You can be put in compromising situations in college; you can be walking around here late at night and something bad can happen. But use common sense and don't be paralyzed by fear.

But in D.C., it's a very real thing. There's a lot of men with power and money, and there's a lot of young women who do go out for that drink, thinking whatever they're thinking, I don't know. Before I went down there, I was like, "Oh it's fairy tale stuff." It's real. I mean, there's a lot of men asking women to go out drinking, and a lot of young women that do go out on these one-on-one dates. I don't know, I don't have the answers to change that or to give them advice, but it's a real problem. It doesn't always turn into an affair, but it happens. And young women should be aware . . . especially going to D.C., although I'm sure it happens in other cities. But politics is funny, you know. You know, they're all excited about going to the Hill. There's a lot of shady stuff that goes on, and young women I think should be aware that it's a real thing that they will be confronted with. So maybe the one advice you can give them is be prepared for when that question does come. And if it never comes, the better. But if it does come, at least you've thought about it, and you've had that conversation with your best friend or your mom, so you feel guilty when either you say yes or you feel good when you say no. You know that you were prepared for that question, because it does happen.

Beth: Not on personal safety, but about being a woman: I found that it's very hard to be patient with a lot of the men calling, because the way they would talk to me made me—the fact that I sound younger, they would just talk down to me. "Can I talk to someone in charge?" Like, "Is there a man there that I can talk to?" I've seriously gotten that a couple of times from different constituents.

Did you tell them that your boss was a woman?

Beth: Yeah, but then they want to talk to our executive aid because they think that person does more. Then I tell them the executive aid is also a woman; they're not very thrilled with that either. But there's so many things involved with being a woman in the workplace, and you should be very patient and controlled.

Any final—and brief—concluding thoughts?

Natalia: I would just say, your experience is what you make it. If you're going to be in an office, use it to your advantage. Try all different things, learn about everything. That way, you're going to realize what you do like and realize what you don't. From working at all my internships, I realized that I don't really enjoy handling constituent complaints, but I am really interested in how the office deals with the press. I'm really interested in long-term projects. One of my projects right now, I'm working to get handicapped access for a post office in [a town]. I like working with the different agencies, like trying to push the project along, more than I would like solving an individual person's problems. But you just have to find your hook, I guess.

Aaron: And while you're trying out everything, just keep an open mind. You just might learn something. Everything that you do can be a learning experience; it just depends on whether you look at it.

You folks are great. Thanks!

Index

Printed in the United States
216425BV00002B/22/A

9 780813 340166